COMMUNITY DEVELOPMENT PRACTICE

STORIES, METHOD AND MEANING

EDITED BY:
ANN INGAMELLS, ATHENA LATHOURAS, ROSS WISEMAN,
PETER WESTOBY, FIONA CANIGLIA

COMMUNITY DEVELOPMENT PRACTICE

STORIES, METHOD AND MEANING

EDITED BY:
ANN INGAMELLS, ATHENA LATHOURAS, ROSS WISEMAN,
PETER WESTOBY, FIONA CANIGLIA

Common Ground

First published in Australia in 2010
by Common Ground Publishing Pty Ltd
at The Social Sciences
a series imprint of The University Press

The National Library of Australia Cataloguing-in-Publication data:

Community development practice stories: method and meaning
Editor: Ann Ingamells ... [et al.]

Includes index.
Bibliography.

978 1 86335 645 9 (pbk.)
978 1 86335 646 6 (pdf)

1. Community development—Australia—Methodology.
2. Community development—Australia—Case studies.
3. Social planning—Australia—Methodology.
4. Social planning—Australia—Case studies.

307.10994

Table of Contents

Foreword x

Acknowledgments xi

Contributors xii

Chapter 1: Community Development 1
Ann Ingamells
Contemporary contexts 5
References 8

Chapter 2: Developmental Community Work - A Method 11
Athena Lathouras
Introduction 11
Founders of the method 12
Philosophical concepts underpinning the method 12
Method of community development 14
At the heart of the method - values and practice principles utilised by
   the Nambour Community Centre 16
Distinguishing features of developmental community work practised
   at the Nambour Community Centre 18
The relational method – from private concerns to public action 21
'o-1-3' - Stories from practice 22
Conclusion 27
References 28

Chapter 3: The Circle of Men Project 29
Ross Wiseman
Part One: The Circle of Men Project 30
Part Two: Social Analysis and Context 35
Part Three: Infrastructure: Fork in the Road 41
References 45

Chapter 4: The Circle of Men 47
Karen Finlay, Mark Creyton and Ann Ingamells
A commentary on Circle of Men 48
Circle of Men – then, now and soon 49
The Circle of Men Project as community capacity building 51

Conclusion 54

References 54

Chapter 5: Story of Working with Southern Sudanese refugees within Brisbane and Logan 57

Peter Westoby

Introduction 57

Background 58

The Sudanese story of coming to Australia 59

Returning to the story 61

Towards a new analysis 64

Giving the analysis legs 66

The on-going story 67

The outcomes and conclusion 69

For Southern Sudanese 69

For organisations 70

For myself as practitioner 70

References 71

Chapter 6: A Sense of a Whole Other World 73

Polly Walker, John Diew, Di Zetlin

Responding to Peter's story and reflecting on my bi-cultural role 74

Building community capacity 74

My role 74

Only a Sudanese worker? 76

Self-care 76

Conclusion 76

A Sense of a Whole Other World: Worldviewing and Ethical Collaboration across Social Worlds 77

Editor's Transition 80

Discovery and dialogue: a reflection on a community development PhD 81

Meeting Peter 81

The role of discovery 82

Theory/Practice 83

Conclusion 84

References 84

Chapter 7: The Search for Invisible Cities 85

Fiona Caniglia

Background 86

About urban renewal in Brisbane 87

Beginning tales 90

Holding the bigger picture: critical social analysis in the context of
   front line practice 92

The challenge of language 93

Listening to stories 94

Bringing people together 95

A clearer focus on structures 97

Time, place, opportunity 99

A pool of tears 100

Building the base 101

Conclusion 103

References 103

Chapter 8: Another Perspective on New Farm Redevelopment 107
Pam Bourke

Chapter 9: Reflexivity Looking Back–! **111**
*Ann Ingamells, Fiona Caniglia, Athena Lathouras, Peter Westoby,
   Ross Wiseman*

References 117

Index of Words **119**

Foreword

It is exciting to see stories emerge based on community development methods that have been taught in Queensland for more than fifty years, starting with Les Halliwell and then given a global perspective by Sugata Dasgupta. I was privileged to inherit this tradition that has been developed and consolidated over the years through the practice and reflection of many community development workers. This tradition remains useful and helpful only in so far as it tested in every-day developmental work. This testing happens best when we take the time to reflect as deeply as we can about the wisdoms of past practice, scrutinise carefully how current work unfolds and finally share with each other a bold vision of what it could be.

A key part of this tradition and a central part of the methodology we use to build and strengthen this work is to share our stories. Sharing stories helps us reflect on the complexities embedded in this work and helps us hold firm to our conviction that when we bring people together in a spirit of listening, learning and adventure, so much becomes possible, even when the pathway is not clear and the tasks to be done anything but straightforward. It is so apparent that our current context brings extraordinary challenges, as we absorb and confront global forces that threaten and sometimes succeed in weakening the bonds between people and the places where they live. For this reason it is particularly important that real stories are told, stories that engage us in dialogue between our values, our thinking and what we ultimately do. Such stories also play an important part in reminding us of the hard-won wisdom learned from previous generations of workers, that guide us when we work to build relationships based on deep listening that can hold up and even flourish against the prevailing tide of the current times.

The honest stories in this book highlight these hopes and tensions, complexities and challenges when we work to build community in the midst of more dominant paradigms. They paint a picture of the power of this work yet also its fragility. These stories highlight how hard it can be to achieve and sustain evidence of success. It therefore becomes important to share ways of working that energise and give us hope, even in the face of apparent failure, especially when we verge on thinking that our successes are too few and failures too many. This book is a wonderful contribution to the story-telling tradition established by Les and Sugata and will find its helpful way into the hearts and minds of the workers who want to continue and be part of the struggle to build better and stronger communities.

Anthony Kelly
Brisbane 2009

Acknowledgments

Ross Wiseman

I would like to thank Michael Tarlo and Washuntara (founders of the Circle of Men) for putting in so many hours with me in sharing what is their story, and for being all round good guys. I have told them they should have their DNA reproduced so that a little bit could be transplanted to all men to make the world that much better a place. Similarly, I express my thanks to Karen Finlay (late of Redland City Council) and Mark Creyton (Volunteering Queensland) for taking time out of their busy schedules to write their informed responses to my chapter.

Athena Lathouras

I would like to acknowledge the many community members and colleagues I have worked with, and the more experienced CD practitioners who have guided me in my practice over the years. Evvalynn Vanderpoel, who was the Chairperson of Nambour Community Centre for many of the years I worked there, supported me, trusted me and we were a great team. Much of the great work that happened there was because of Evvalynn's leadership and vision for community.

Dr Peter Westoby

I am deeply indebted to so many un-named people within the Brisbane and Logan Sudanese community. However, I'd like to particularly acknowledge and name John Diew, Uncle Gabriel, Uncle Choul, Dhano, Jacob, Daniel, Gabriel, Juba and Edward. With regards to those supporting me in my journey with refugees I'd like to thank Carolyn Cox, Paula Peterson, Donata Rossi, Dave & Angie Andrews and Carlos Monterosa.

Fiona Caniglia

I am eternally grateful to everyone associated with New Farm Neighbourhood Centre for the extent of my learning as a worker. Thanks especially to successive management committees, Maida Lilley, John Coyle, Keith Hancox, Ron Muir, Joe Neal, Rob Thompson and Gordon Fredericks for hanging in there despite the odds. Stephen Dowling embodied for me the full impacts of urban renewal, and shaped much of my practice without ever really knowing it.

We are all very grateful to our families who have supported us with love and patience to grow as people and in our work. We would all especially like to thank Ann Ingamells for having the vision and leadership to take us forward in publishing this book.

Contributors

Ann Ingamells

Dr Ann Ingamells is a Senior Lecturer in the School of Human Services and Social Work at Griffith University. As well as teaching community development, Ann involves students in a range of community development activities and assists organisations with their community work. She contributes to the promotion of community work in Queensland via the network Community Development Queensland.

Ross Wiseman

Ross Wiseman has worked in a variety of roles, organisations and places in the community services sector. He has taught in community development in TAFE, involving his students in rolling research and community development projects in partnership with many local NGOs and local government. In retirement, Ross can still be found actively involved in the consolidation of smaller housing organisations into larger growth providers. He is also engaged with PeakCare Queensland in developing some exciting strategies for the long term sustainability of small NGOs in the State.

Athena (Tina) Lathouras

Athena Lathouras (B.Soc.Wk; Grad Cert Soc Wk [Com Dev]) has worked in the social services sector since 1980 in the areas of: disability services, neighbourhood centres and peak bodies. She is currently a full-time student undertaking doctoral studies at the University of Queensland, investigating community development and structural dimensions of disadvantage and practice.

Dr Peter Westoby

Dr Peter Westoby is currently a Lecturer in Community Development in the School of Social Work & Human Services and an Honorary Research Fellow with the Australian Centre for Peace & Conflict Studies (ACPACS) at the University of Queensland. He is also a Director with Community Praxis Co-op. Peter Westoby has over 20 years of experience in refugee related work, youth work practice and community development. He has worked in South Africa, Papua New Guinea, the Philippines, Vanuatu and Australia.

Fiona Caniglia

Fiona's background is in social work, community development and community planning. After an early career in acute mental health, Fiona worked for New Farm Neighbourhood Centre in various roles between 1994 and 2006. Fiona has also worked on housing and homelessness issues for a variety of agencies (government and non-government) and is currently working for diverse NGOs, government agencies and universities on projects, research and writing while staying actively involved in her own neighbourhood.

Mark Creyton

Mark Creyton is Manager, Education, Research and Policy at Volunteering Queensland. He has over twenty years experience as an educator and consultant working with volunteer and non profit groups. His particular interest is the role of such groups in creating a strong and vital civil society.

Karen Finlay

Karen Finlay holds a Bachelor of Social Science (Human Services), A Diploma of Counselling and is a full member of the Australian Institute of Welfare and Community Workers Inc. Karen met Ross through her work with the Redlands Advisory Group on Seniors Issues (RAGOSI). She says their paths crossed often and although she encountered the Circle of Men through her work, the comments in her paper are her own observations and words. Karen was the primary author of Ageing Well in the Redlands: a ten year strategy for seniors, adopted by Redland Shire Council in 2006 and referred to in the case study.

Di Zetlin

In addition to her academic work at the University of Queensland, Di Zetlin has worked in a variety of professional jobs, including the Bertrand Russell Peace Foundation, and has been the General Secretary of the trade union representing academic staff.

Polly O. Walker

Polly Walker is of Cherokee and settler American descent and grew up in New Mexico. At the time of writing she was a post doctoral fellow at the Australian Centre for Peace and Conflict Studies, University of Queensland.

John Diew

John Kor Diew, BA, MA, was born in 1966 in Ulang, in Upper Nile State, Southern Sudan. He took active part in armed struggle in Sudan from July 1984 to August 1998. He resettled to Australia under Humanitarian Program in Sept 1998 and acquired Australian citizenship in 2000. He obtained Bachelor of Arts in Politics and Government from Griffith University (August 2002) in Australia and Master of Social Administration in the University of Queensland (December 2005). From 2002 to 2005 he worked in Brisbane as an advocate for a Non Government organisation. He went back to Sudan in 2005 and was appointed as State Secretary for Sudan People's Liberation Movement (SPLM) in Upper Nile State in Southern Sudan. He was democratically elected to the same position in 2008 which he is currently serving the SPLM.

Pam Bourke

Pam Bourke has extensive experience in working with local and state governments at a senior level to broker policy change and strategic partnerships in Australia and New Zealand. She is highly experienced in community engagement and community development both in terms of leading policy and strategy and in developing and managing community engagement projects and processes in complex and conflictual environments. Pam has recently developed and delivered two courses in community development and engagement for the Mining Industry.

Chapter 1
Community Development

Traditions of Practice and Contemporary Contexts

Ann Ingamells

> *Why does one write about community? For whom? With whom? In the midst of what company? From inside what collectivity? Given what traditions? From what "location"? Given what self understandings? ... To what extent is the writing one's own map for the direction of movement? How many voices can one hear in the writing/planning?*

Lugones (1998, p. 466).

Twenty years ago, Kelly & Sewell began their book about community building by saying:

> *Writing this book, we have been conscious of the lifetimes of human experience that have shaped what we now understand community building to mean (1988, p. 2).*

The editors of this book begin with a similar sentiment. We see in our practice the traces of the many: people, colleagues, mentors, educators, community stories, practitioner accounts, that have influenced us over many years, yet we also recognise at the heart of our practice, a tradition, that we colloquially call 'a developmental approach'. This book is a collection of narratives and commentaries through which we hope to both make this 'tradition' evident and nurture its continuance, whilst recognising that tradition is never enough, is partial and is contested.

Any story, told by one or more narrators, is limited in the possible levels of meaning it can locate itself at and convey. Personal experience, method, technique, purpose, practice orientation, organisational context, funding regimes, conflicting agendas, competing philosophies can be revealed or eclipsed. Each story reflects *a* telling rather than *the* telling. New dimensions of the story can be brought out by different tellings from people differently positioned, and/or by reading it through one of many possible lenses. Each chapter of this book that tells a story is followed by a commentary chapter that brings different or additional readings to what is going on.

By way of introduction, this chapter considers the nature of a tradition of practice and the elements of this particular tradition. Chapter two unpacks further components of the approach. This chapter also considers the ways in which a tradition of practice changes in response and reaction to shifts in the socio economic and political environment.

The term 'tradition' has several meanings. We use it loosely here to mean an orientation, an intellectual heritage, a set of values and assumptions and a cluster of particular practices that hang together and are sustained by a group of people, in our case, in a particular place, over time (Hope-Simpson & Westoby, 2009). Traditions are often influenced by schools of thought centred in, and taught from, universities over a period of time.

The intellectual and philosophical traces of this particular approach to community work are from people-centred humanist traditions (such as Buber, 1965), non violent schools of social action, such as discussed by Gandhi, (Fischer, 1962) and emancipatory schools of thought such as Freire (1997) and Illich (1973). The practice tradition emphasises change driven by community members from the bottom up, in a way that brings private concerns to the public world and democratically negotiates the terms of change between diverse groups. The normative distinction of the developmental approach resides in the conceptualisation of who the primary actors are and how change happens. This tradition positions community members (rather than workers) as the primary actors, beginning with the poorest, most marginal, disadvantaged or those most affected by adverse policies. Change is pursued through relationships and through the transformative power of dialogue. The practices include equipping the actors for their role in change and creating the kinds of structures that enable and sustain participation and bottom up agendas and decision making.

The method at the core of the approach begins with the horizontal linking of person to person, group to group, through dialogue and conviviality (community building) (Westoby & Dowling, 2009). Aspirations of the group are expressed through existing, changed or new structures to the public world. Analysis and reflection indicate the trajectory of change, and facilitate new patterns of thought and action. Strategies vary between creating alternatives, bringing new people/energies/ideas to old forms, through dialogue across power differentials confronting issues and seeking new solutions, negotiation, lobbying, campaigning and as a last resort seeking to apply pressure on resistant and entrenched interests, albeit within respectful and non violent ways.

Even within the developmental tradition there have always been differences of emphasis between identifiable groups. Some groups stayed closer to the horizontal work, committed in their communities to building solidarity with people who are usually marginalised and excluded (Andrews, 1996). Other groups moved more to the work at the intersection of vertical (social structures) and horizontal (community relations) emphasising the effort to bring about wider changes that make institutions more responsive to community articulated need and aspiration (Daveson, 2000). Between these have been those with a place base, or specific group focus, both concerned to enhance residents identity with a place, fostering awareness and resident voice to secure better resources and supports for a range of groups, mindful always of the least advantaged, in a local place.

Community development is embedded in many disciplines of practice from agriculture and environment through nursing, rehabilitation, engineering and planning, education, sports, recreation and arts. Perhaps one of its most familiar homes has been social work. Connie Benn (1981) is often credited as the practitioner who first gave a clear articulation of the developmental approach in social work, yet her critique is relevant to many professions and most public servants. Her observation was that professionals tend to set up a situation in which the power stays in the worker's hands, and therefore the worker remains in control. When it came to more empowering ways of working, she argued that such professionals know very little 'about redistribution of resources, participation techniques, consumerism, or even how to change social structures' (1981, p. 92). Professionals, she claimed, acted as if the cause of poverty or disadvantage lay in the personal defects of individuals.

Benn argued for a developmental approach which has three aspects:

1. Social change can only be achieved if a group has four kinds of power -
   - power over resources
   - power over relationships
   - power over information
   - power over decision making.

2. The techniques to obtain these powers are - participation strategies, self help mechanisms and deprofessionalisation.

3. The following elements are essential to the approach -
   - that it be directed to change in society's institutions, rather than change in individuals
   - that it be resource-oriented, rather than problem oriented

- that it lead to self-actualisation, rather than to stigmatisation of the individual
- that it be a means of social change and not a means of social control
- that life choices be made freely by participation, and not imposed by professionals
- that professional workers be accountable to community and consumers and not to their peers
- that decisions be made by participants
- that individuals determine their own life-styles, rather than having their lifestyles decided by discriminatory and discretionary provisions.

Benn was clearly talking about an approach to professional practice which has been built on over the years to include empowerment, anti-discriminatory and strength based approaches. Yet, whilst the theory is increasingly espoused and articulated, practices in the field often make less headway. In the narratives of this text, community members continue to encounter many barriers to determining their own lifestyles, practitioners continue to find it difficult to engage people in a sustainable way and organisations find themselves concerned more with control than empowerment.

The strong functionalist underpinning of western society has a predisposition to identifying a problem and acting to fix it. This is what Kelly & Sewell call a linear approach. It relies on binary thinking which positions the problem as out there, usually in 'the system' and quite separate from the people experiencing it. Kelly & Sewell (1988) argue that life is always more complicated than this. They say the developmental process counters this cultural tendency towards linear expression, through processes that are cyclical, multi dimensional in thought, action and relationship. In this journey, a professional needs to learn to work alongside the people, knowing that no one can do the journey for another, and that readiness and capacity for change will develop over time, and that the goal of the action will change along the way. Expanding how one thinks is a crucial part of this developmental journey:

> To build community, we need to be able to work with many different kinds of people, organisational structures and action emphases. We also need to be able to ... expand our thinking to more than one pattern...Locked into one logic or pattern of thinking, we make and accept judgements solely on the basis of what is familiar, whereas with an open mind we are open to both new ideas and to the way we process those ideas.

(Kelly & Sewell, 1988, p. 12)

The developmental approach then is about shifts in power, in thinking and in personal and social agency. It combines the logic of horizontal relationship building, person to person in the community, with the logic of relating from the horizontal to the vertical structures of society. Carmel Daveson (1996, 2000) has been key to the articulation of these quite distinct movements. The movement from private to public requires firstly the relationships between community members and secondly, when agreements are clear and the group is ready, the shift to relating structurally. For Daveson (1996), however, the shift to relating structurally is not a shift to adversary mode. She, like Kelly & Sewell (1988) view the kind of binary thinking which posits us against the system, as outside the developmental approach. The developmental approach takes a relationship building approach to change and the challenge is always to see how far the process can go by working on and within the relationships whether along horizontal or vertical axes.

Not all proponents of the developmental approach are against adversary measures, rather they see them as a measure to be taken when all efforts to bring about change through developmental and democratic processes have failed. The developmental approach pushes the democratic process as far as it can be pushed through relationships, dialogue, and negotiation. It connects horizontal to vertical informally through existing relationships and through formal channels. It applies pressure through concepts of fairness, justice, human rights, better governance, better value for money, more finely attuned policy and so on.

As such, the developmental approach, as Daveson (1996) points out, may be more akin to a social movement than a professional or even grass roots activity. Indeed, those who embrace the developmental method tend to advocate bringing the whole self to the process, as opposed to fragmenting the self across professional and other roles (Andrews, 1996; Daveson, 1996; Tennant, 2000). There is evidence of this too in the narratives that follow. When the formal work pathways are blocked, practitioners maintain the convivial after work relations, and they seek other ways of continuing the trajectory outside of work, for example by research or other collaborations.

This book grows out of such a tradition, but whilst the past may inform current practice, it does not constitute it. The stories show how people draw eclectically on a range of resources to respond to or shape the moment. Hopefully the stories indicate that a tradition can guide practice, but a tradition or approach is not something that can be *applied*. Context is never inert, relationship dynamics are complex, and responding to a given set of dynamics is less about getting it right and more about making choices, acting within constraints and sustaining momentum.

Contemporary contexts

Throughout the 1970s and 1980s, community workers found some compatibilities between their method of approach, community people's willingness to get involved and the willingness of government and other authorities to engage with communities. Social justice provided the discourse of rights and access, fairness, equity, and participation. Always imperfect, there was nevertheless enough fit between the developmental approach and the broader political philosophy to provide leverage for some change. But gradually the socio political context was changing. Community infrastructure was being professionalised through delivery of welfare services. Managerial mechanisms of standards, accreditation, accounting mechanisms and risk management were making it more difficult for paid workers to engage bottom up with people. Insurance companies required volunteers to have job descriptions and tighter attachment to service delivery goals. People were constructed as either clients, consumers or volunteers; community members began to disappear from the available subject positions. Advocacy became high risk for funding approval and the networks of agencies that had supported each other's community efforts were being positioned as competitors. Instead of community organisations being a mechanism through which communities had a voice, they had become part of the bureaucratic chain of service delivery.

One might imagine that communities and their workers would be angry, resistant and outspoken about these shifts. Some have been, and most also see that they are in some ways complicit with the new agendas. The creeping parallel force of consumer, market oriented individualism, has somehow redefined the good citizen as the person who provides their own private housing, superannuation, healthcare, training and children's private school education. Few of us remain unaffected by this collapse of collectivism in favour of market-individualism. Community work effort then seemed to battle encroaching forces with little groundswell of wider support. As some opportunities for community work closed off, however, there appeared to be new openings.

Urban and community renewal, along with place management, were emerging as new government programs of engaging communities. These seemed to offer new and exciting opportunities for communities to participate. It transpired, after some time, that community engagement meant people from the community getting involved in making government agendas work. It meant government engaging with business and corporations. It meant that communities were being transformed by 'development' agendas that were not their own. Community held agendas became more difficult to articulate and sustain. Community members whose interests were served by the new agendas (e.g. their own property values might increase) got involved; those whose interests were not served, voted with their feet. This drove a further wedge between those with and those without resources in each community, with the least advantaged pushed further to the margins (Ingamells, 2007).

Industrial conditions within the community sector have added to the challenges. Community work remains the most poorly paid of the social professions, with those working at the local level least resourced. There are no senior positions for community workers, despite the complexity of the work. To move up the ladder is to move into management positions. So, potential community workers have to make hard decisions. Sometimes paying the mortgage and feeding the family take precedence. This then is a low point from which to reflect on the work. However, the stories indicate some of the ways workers are engaging with the challenges, reorganising their personal and community lives to hold in with the issues, move sideways to include other kinds of activities in their broader repertoire of work and drawing on the literature to sustain, what is often pointed out, that contesting the status quo never comes easily.

The shift to consumerism and market affects us all. We become: less likely to recreate in local community groups and more likely to go to the gym; less likely to improvise music in a participatory way and more likely to consume or provide market based experiences; less likely to care for each other's children and more likely to use private childcare; less likely to shop locally and more likely to choose the Westfield shopping mall. Whilst it may be that community building does occur within gym, private school and even shopping mall, nevertheless we become less invested in the well being of the wider collective, the links between us become obscured, and cynicism about the relevance of community takes hold.

Even as the ties of collectivity are obscured by the rhetoric of individualism and consumer choice through the market, we remain firmly and inevitably connected to each other and to the planet. We are connected through the social arrangements made for the care of our children, their education and their safety in parks, streets and other facilities, the quality of our healthcare, the infrastructure through which our working life is shaped, the security of our superannuation investments, and the quality of arrangements for our old age. We are connected through the internet, media and telecommunication to an interdependency which exceeds anything which has gone before. We are connected through our mutual dependence upon the ozone layer, oceans, air, water, ice caps and biosphere of our planet (Burkett, 1998).

Of course, many community groups have emerged in reaction to these global changes and in response to these contemporary ways that we are connected. People are expressing alternative values through minimising consumption, buying locally, becoming active around climate change, shifting gender roles, changing lifestyles and habits to express the changes they would like to see. These are however happening at a social distance from those places where disadvantage is most prevalent. Meanwhile as more people are excluded from broader social processes and seek support at the local level, funding goes increasingly to large non government or private organisations that have little attachment to, or presence in, place.

A tradition of practice inherits ideas from the past – truths that were shaped by past conditions. To defend core beliefs against change, is to become irrelevant to living in the present. Only through stories can we discern the continuities and discontinuities of tradition as it informs present practice. Each instance of practice then is a determined effort to take the accumulated wisdom of the past and transform it through action in the present. In this way, people come to know the way their world works, and add to their tools and tradition as the present demands. The guiding force of the tradition becomes the stake around which new understandings and practices gravitate, and in our tradition, this is to value and nurture the impetus to recognise, acknowledge, affirm, enable, animate, and skill-up, those parts of all of us which care for the people and places and circumstances of which we ourselves are a small part.

The narratives of this book, are all set in this context of globalisation, managerialism and individualism. Agents, external to the local community, in each story want to harness community energy in the name of some agenda of their own. The external agenda and the internal agenda sit uncomfortably together, with many of the resources on the external side. Practitioners of this space between what is internal to a community and what external agents want of it, are working on many fronts at once to build and sustain connections. There is a pressure to tell simplified success stories of practice, but the narrators have resisted this pressure. The stories show the struggle, the effort, the learning and the varied feelings that accompany the work. Each of the story narrators is on a journey, stepping into and out of the fray. The learning goes on and in a sense, none of the stories is finished.

The risk is that people will read these narratives and think it is all too hard. We hope the book will encourage people towards greater involvement, not because the stories promise success, but because they matter. We hope people will be encouraged to nurture the efforts of themselves and others to contribute to collective life, 'as if people mattered', and as if all people mattered equally. And, we might add, as, Jim Ife (2002) did, as if all people understood how interrelated people and planet are. We live in a dynamic, complicated, multi-layered world, where injustice persists and conscious efforts at change are hard wrought. Yet, equally we live in a world of people, ideas and resources to assist transformation. We hope this book will encourage people to step into the more complex areas of practice and share their successes, disappointments and learning along the way.

References

Andrews, D. (1996). *Building a better world*. Sutherland, N.S.W.: Albatross.

Benn, C. (1981). Innovation in welfare programmes. In R.F. Henderson (Ed.), *The welfare stakes* (pp. 84-105). Melbourne: Melbourne University Press.

Buber, M. (1965) *Between man and man*. New York: Macmillan.

Burkett, I. (1998). *Thinking, acting, linking globally from the local community: A community development response to the local global nexus*. PhD Thesis, University of Queensland.

Daveson, C. (1996). *Finding a voice: Towards the naming of a social change framework*. Masters Thesis, University of Queensland.

Daveson, C. (2000). From private concern to public action. *Culture Matters, 1*, 38-41.

Fischer, L. (1962). *The essential Gandhi*. New York: Random House.

Freire, P. (1997). *Pedagogy of the heart*. (transl. D. Macedo & A. Oliviera with notes by Ana Freire). A.M.A. New York: Continuum.

Hope-Simpson, G. & Westoby, P. (2009). Unpublished paper, *Traditions and community development: A literature review*. Community Development Unit, University of Queensland.

Ife, J. (2002). *Community development: Creating community alternatives – vision, analysis and practice*. Melbourne, Longman.

Illich, I. (1973). *Tools for conviviality*. London: Calder & Boyars.

Ingamells, A. (2007). Community development and community renewal: Tracing the workings of power. *Community Development Journal*, *42*(2), 237-250.

Kelly, A. & Sewell, S. (1988). *With head, heart & hand: Dimensions of community building*. Brisbane: Boolarong Press.

Maria Lugones. (1998). Community. In A. Jagger & I.M.Young, (Eds). *A companion to feminist philosophy*. Massachusetts: Blackwell.

Tennant, M. (2000). *From Madonna to Medusa: The revision of community work in the light of the revision of the self*. Masters Thesis, University of Queensland.

Westoby, P. & Dowling, G. (2009). *Dialogical community development: With depth, solidarity and hospitality*. Brisbane: Tafina.

Chapter 2
Developmental Community Work - A Method

Athena Lathouras

Introduction

I am one of the graduates from the University of Queensland's (UQ) School of Social Work and Human Services. Like many other Queensland practitioners, I owe much to the work of Anthony Kelly who taught community development and related subjects over a 25-year period. Anthony's contribution to the field of community development ignited the flame of my imagination when he taught me a unique developmental approach that can be used to create a socially just world. This approach to community development practice is about working with small groups to build their capacity to do whatever is needed for active citizenship and full participation in society. It requires action that is strategic and proactive with the aim of reducing or preventing the deleterious effects of oppressive systems and structures.

For the past twelve years I have been working in paid and unpaid community development contexts, most recently at Nambour Community Centre in the Sunshine Coast Hinterland. This chapter describes the philosophical traditions that have contributed to the method, the particular values and practice principles in which it is firmly rooted, and some of the distinguishing features of the approach. It also describes my interpretation of the developmental approach to community work and how we have been applying it at the Nambour Community Centre and in the wider Sunshine Coast these past few years.

Founders of the method

The developmental method, used by many in Queensland, has been articulated and expanded upon by past UQ lecturers and practitioners: Les Halliwell, Sugata Dasgupta, Anthony Kelly and Ingrid Burkett.

The developmental approach is sometimes referred to as the 'Gandhian tradition' of community building, referring to links with Mohandas K Gandhi and his position on non-violence to achieve democratic socialism. Dasgupta (1974, p.34) articulated Gandhi's definition of violence as 'exploitation, centralisation of power and dominance; all that retards free expression of the weak who live at the base of society'. Gandhi's fundamental analysis was that if he pursued the truth of the matter, known as Satyagraha – the force of truth, that exploitation and dominance creates poverty; then this would unleash the most powerful moral, social and economic forces available to rectify oppression (Kelly, 2005). In the Gandhian tradition the development process is based on truth, not power, to be a force of liberation for the 'poorest of the poor'.

Philosophical concepts underpinning the method

The philosophical concepts embedded in this method are not new. However, the way they have been articulated together has created a unique, practical and disciplined approach to community development work. This approach has been utilised by practitioners in many locations and contexts, both in Australian settings and in global south contexts. The method has been influenced by a number of philosophers and educators including Rabindranath Tagore, Martin Buber and Paulo Freire. The concepts they espoused and how these have been used within the method will now be discussed.

Making connections

Rabindranath Tagore, a poet, philosopher and Nobel Prize winner for literature, suggested a foundational principle for establishing developmental relationships: that is, to make a connection, one has to 'see through the eyes of another'. Tagore (1861-1941) was born into a wealthy Bengali family and managed his father's rural estates. Many poor people lived and worked around these estates. As he became sensitive to their hardships, he asked them how he could help. Their response was that he could not begin to understand their life of struggle because he had come from such a different world (Kelly, 2008). With this insight, Tagore laid the foundation for this approach, one that questions the typical stance of 'helper as expert'. It begins from a premise that a helper, rather than having expert knowledge, is the learner (Andrews, 2004). The helper does not understand what is best for the community, or what could be done in a particular situation. Rather, this wisdom must come from those living in these situations. This understanding establishes a quality of mutuality within the relationships. To see through the eyes of another is to put aside the helper's notion of what is to be done, and truly understand the other's point of view. This stance, that values learning about the experience of another, is an important first step in the development process.

Dialogue – three movements

Martin Buber (1878-1965) was a prolific writer, educator and philosopher. From his influential philosophy of Dialogue, described in 'I and Thou' (1937) the second principle of the developmental method was derived. Buber's thesis differentiated between 'I-Thou' and 'I-It' relationships. Of these, the I-Thou depicts the relationship between man (sic) and the world as one of mutuality, openness, and directness. Buber's contribution to the method builds from Tagore's wisdom. To truly see through the eyes of another, relationships hinge on the quality of the dialogue that occurs between people. Meaningful dialogue takes place when mutual understanding about particular matters is established between those involved.

Buber identified three connected and enfolding 'movements' in our dialogue with others (Kelly, 2008). 'First movement' interaction occurs when we present ourselves to another and say who we are and why we are here. 'Second movement' dialogue occurs when there is a response from the other to our first movement statements or questions. 'Third movement' dialogue is our response to their response. It requires us to be attentive to what is being said, to listen for and connect with the data or content they are communicating. Attaining third movement is not easy, especially because, in the desire to help, one usually finds it difficult to set aside one's particular agenda and truly connect dialogically.

Genuine dialogue, such as suggested by Buber, necessarily goes through all three movements, folding one into another, back and forth in a reciprocal fashion. Buber describes this process of establishing mutual or developmental relationships as moving from 'I' (first movement) to 'You' (second movement) to 'We' (third movement) (Westoby & Owen, 2009). 'Community' has been described as the sum of the mutual relationships between people. Buber's respectful dialogical framework, which values mutuality, is at the heart of this approach to community development work.

Listening for key words to build action

Paulo Freire (1921-1997), Brazilian educator and philosopher in the late 20th Century, suggested that during dialogue we listen for and explore 'generative themes' (1970, p.77), to build action. This concept forms the third foundational principle of the method. Creating genuine dialogue gives us vast amounts of data about people's lives, concerns, hopes and dreams. To make sense of this data and to guide purposeful action, we need to be strategic in our dialogical endeavours. Heurisms are words that evoke a particular meaning for both the speaker and the listener (Kelly & Sewell, 1988). Everyday words like 'community', 'family', 'work', are all heurisms. Each of us attaches meaning to heurisms according to, amongst other things, our life experience; our educational backgrounds; and personal frameworks through which we view the world. Connecting in third movement dialogue requires us to explore heurisms to establish the other's meaning of those key words. This is truly what is meant by the 'gift of listening'.

Heuristic logic is used in many disciplines. Child development specialists use 'heuristic play' when working with children to explore what playing with a particular toy means for a child. Therapists, when counselling, listen for particular heurisms regarding a person's emotional state. The heurisms to which community development practitioners attend are those considered to be 'action-reflection' heurisms. These are usually verbs or keywords that lend themselves to some sort of action.

For example, a number of heurisms are apparent in the following statement: 'I've been feeling pretty annoyed about the situation, but now I think it's time to get involved'. The action-reflection heurism is 'involved'. A third movement question back to this speaker would be, 'In what ways do you think you should get involved?' or 'What does getting involved mean to you?' Further exploration of their response might elicit ideas for action that would be in step with their hopes, dreams and desires.

In summary, the three principles outlined in this section are: making connections by seeing through the eyes of another; building relationships through dialogue, and mobilising action by listening for keywords. Together these create the basis upon which this developmental method is enacted. It is a method in which the people affected by the particular circumstance are integral to all aspects of the development process. Such an approach requires a shift in thinking from the practitioner doing something *for* or *to* people, to doing something *with* people.

Method of community development

Method is the way in which we organise our engagement in the work, including the processes and procedures we use, the systems we encounter and the intentions we have which underpin our practice. There are several dimensions of the method, including: implicate-method; micro-method;

mezzo-method; macro-method and meta-method. It should be noted that although written as a categorical list below, these methodological approaches are inherent within each other. For instance, implicate-method and micro-method are present and applied in the other methodological domains. Furthermore, a worker might be required to enter the work through any of these domains. For example, if they join in with a previously established macro-method process, they will be drawing on other methodological domains at the same time as engaging in the macro-method process.

Implicate-method is where practitioners position themselves into the work assertively and intentionally. It moves the worker beyond generic job descriptions and methodically and reflexively explores the worker's unique and individual voice in the work (Kelly, 2008). The practitioner explores their self-view and their world-view. They acknowledge who they are and where they have come from. This process links to their capacity to join with others, and to ground the work in the midst of complexity. This is sometimes referred to as a practitioner's explicit framework for practice.
For all, practitioners and community members alike, this reflection helps us understand how our internal world shapes the work or our actions, in the external world.

Micro-method is when the worker joins with others, and assists those people to hear each other's stories, seeing what they see, engaging in dialogue and working with reflective action themes that enable social change. They do this because they are concerned with the agendas of the people and with the sustainability and mutuality of process. This process is sometimes referred to as 'bonding'.

Mezzo-method is the process of moving from the private concern of individuals into public action with others; or when a group with its issues, connects to the structures in society. For example, a group of parents work with a public institution, such as a school, to progress particular issues they have in common about their children in the school context. The worker facilitates and supports these processes. Sometimes referred to as 'banding', because people band together to take action for social change. Workers engage with groups of people in such a way that participants appreciate their points of connection, make decisions and take mutually beneficial action. The aim of mezzo-method is to build self-help and mutual aid amongst participants, by establishing: a shared agenda, a shared basis for working together, and a shared commitment to follow through with the action/s - sometimes referred to as having a 'community analysis'.

Macro-method is when workers nurture partner relationships in the form of community organisations. This is both as an expression of community itself and an instrumental mechanism to achieve the public purpose of the organisation. Community development processes build organisations that are community-based and community-owned. The aim is to build organisations and social infrastructure to achieve a public good. This process is sometimes referred to as 'structuring the work', or establishing mechanisms that enable community development work to be sustained.

Meta-method occurs when practitioners facilitate community development processes to join with others who are doing this work and integrate both locally and globally. Progressive community development theorists, whose thoughts are often shaped by a global analysis of poverty, argue for a practice that makes local and global connections; or at least a practice that is informed by a global analysis, and then attempts to go beyond the local. Meta-method acknowledges the complexities and paradoxes of this work and is when coalitions of macro organisations band together, so that small scale and local work can connect with 'people's movements' for social and global change.

At the heart of the method - values and practice principles utilised by the Nambour Community Centre

Good practice has its roots firmly located within core values (ideals we hold) and practice principles (ways in which we are committed to act). From these values and principles, all developmental practice flows. Practitioners can find the complexities of community work very challenging. This can be because of the great variety of contexts in which we work; the numerous practice approaches that abound; the various and fragmented theoretical underpinnings and the social policy contexts that inform the work; and also the diverse language that is used to discuss practice. Community development work is very 'process-driven'. Frequently, outcomes cannot be prescribed, nor predicted. This can leave a practitioner unsure of which path to take with a particular piece of work. Therefore, it is essential for workers to remain firmly tethered to the core values and principles of community development, which provide guidance for good practice. Below are the values and practice principles given particular attention to by the Nambour Community Centre. These have guided our practice and helped us make decisions about what to focus on and put our energies into.

Underpinning values

Human Dignity and Worth – We believe that every human being has a unique worth; and each person has a right to well-being, self-fulfilment and self-determination, consistent with the rights of others.

Integrality / Involvement - We believe that each individual is an integral member of the community and through their involvement in community activities can realise their personal potential.

Belonging - We believe that when people have a sense of belonging and connection to others, they can experience empowerment. This sense of belonging occurs when people are valued and acknowledged for their unique contribution.

Reconciliation - We acknowledge Aboriginal and Torres Strait Islander peoples as the first peoples of Australia. We are committed to working for reconciliation and justice for Aboriginal and Torres Strait Islander peoples and their land. We are also committed to working in partnership with the local Indigenous community to foster understanding and build positive relationships.

Cultural Diversity - We acknowledge the considerable disadvantages people from culturally and linguistically diverse backgrounds face as migrants, refugees or asylum seekers to Australia. We are committed to providing a voice for people disenfranchised within the community by raising awareness, being an advocate and by providing accessible and equitable services.

Social Justice - We are committed to working for a just society for all its members. Working for social justice encompasses the following: the satisfaction of basic human needs; the equitable distribution of resources to meet these needs; fair access to public services and benefits to achieve human potential; recognition of individuals and community rights and duties; equal treatment and protection under the law; social development and environmental management in the interests of human welfare.

Practice principles

Cooperation – We aim to: develop trust between parties; elicit a commitment from stakeholders to work interdependently; and work together to achieve something collectively. In this way, ideas are generated and participants have a sharper focus on collective outcomes they wish to achieve together.

Partnerships - We endeavour to work with individuals, groups and organisations in partnerships that are based on relationships of trust, mutuality and cooperation.

Sharing Resources - We aim to share our resources that will strengthen and empower a broad range of community activities.

Education - We value the gifts of knowledge and wisdom that individuals bring to any community activity. We also aim to provide opportunities for personal and professional development through access to training or other forms of education. We practise from an educative stance, one that builds understanding, knowledge, and skills that can be applied in all community endeavours.

Accountability / Transparency - We aim to conduct our activities in ways that are transparent, remaining accountable to all our constituents: members, service users, partners, funding bodies, and ourselves.

Responsiveness - We aim to be responsive to community need by providing dynamic and flexible services. We respond by providing a comprehensive information and referral system, and through community development processes we also develop new initiatives and responses when gaps in community services are evident.

Pro-activity - We aim to work with a focus on prevention and early-intervention within the community. Therefore, we will be the instigators of projects that focus on building social capital within the community. 'Social Capital' means the 'glue' or processes between people, which establish networks, norms and social trust and facilitates coordination and cooperation for mutual benefit.

Sustainability - We aim to create sustainable outcomes in the work we conduct to reduce the need for ongoing service delivery. Sustainability refers to the maintenance of the cultural, economic, physical and social wellbeing of people and communities.

Integrity – We value and aim to practise with honesty, reliability and impartiality.

Good Process – Our work aims to encompass good process as its touchstone. We believe 'the means justifies the ends', and not the reverse.

Distinguishing features of developmental community work practised at the Nambour Community Centre

The features outlined below have been described in relation to: *who* is involved in this work; *where* this work occurs; *how* the work is conducted; and *what* the outcomes or desired results are from the work.

Who is involved in this work?

The work is driven by people at the 'grassroots', that is, community members. In this regard, it is considered 'bottom-up' work, not 'top-down' work. Bottom-up work happens when community members set the agenda, the way the work will be undertaken and any other decision-making processes that affect them. This contrasts with the more typical top-down approach, which is one that is primarily driven by workers, often with set agendas and seeking set outcomes which have been instigated by a particular government / social policy agenda.

Community development work undertaken at Nambour Community Centre is referred to as 'developmental community work'. The word 'developmental' can be substituted for the word 'relational', emphasising the importance of good relationship development in the process. The beauty of placing emphasis on relationships means that work undertaken does not necessarily rely on any external resources. People and their relationships with each other are the most valuable resource and are the starting point for any work.

At the Nambour Community Centre a 'whole-of-community' approach to community development work is taken. Individual projects are not targeted towards particular groups 'at risk', as is the case in service provision. Usually, community development projects are open to all who wish to engage. However, one of the features of neighbourhood centre work generally is that it occurs with people who are considered disadvantaged or from particular vulnerable populations. This is an important aspect of the community development work, as often the demands on a worker's time come from a broad cross-section of the community. Generally speaking, Nambour Community Centre workers connect with people who are less resourced or those Gandhi referred to as 'the poorest of the poor'.

Where this work occurs

Developmental community work occurs in the public realm, not the private realm. This compares with other forms of social work / human services work, which mostly occurs with individuals or, for instance, within a 'case management' framework, with families or young people. Interests, concerns, and issues in people's lives are moved from the private realm (individual work) to the public realm (group work), by bringing people together who have similar interests utilising a method, which is referred to as the '0-1-3' (Westoby & Owen, 2009). The 0-1-3 will be explored more thoroughly further on.

This approach to community development work aims to create 'multiple pathways in and out' for participants. 'Multiple pathways in' means creating opportunities for people to connect with others, the worker, and the project, in a range of different ways to work on the concerns they as a collective may have. 'Multiple pathways out', means that the work undertaken creates new and additional opportunities or options for action that people can utilise and move into. This is referred to as having 'agency', because it means having real choices and the ability to act on those choices (Bhattacharyya, 2004). This contrasts with more traditional forms of service delivery, which usually only offer one pathway into an activity / service, and one pathway out, that is, when a participant's involvement with a service is completed they are taken 'off the books'.

How the work is conducted

There is a beautiful saying from Mahatma Ghandi 'carry your agenda lightly'. This means there are multiple ways to build community, and carrying our agenda *lightly* requires that the community itself, not the workers, determine the specifics associated with the work. What we hold onto *tightly* is more of an aim; it is broad. For example, we may have an aim to 'increase community wellbeing' (that is, a sense of happiness and satisfaction with one's life); or to 'create sustainable development', or to 'build stronger communities'. The Nambour Community Centre's motto is apt here, 'Building Community by Working Together'.

This approach is not about service delivery, which ostensibly is about workers, usually from some field of expertise, delivering a particular service to many different people. Each piece of developmental community work is unique and usually not replicable, because it is driven by the particular people who are actors in particular situations and localities. The community development practitioner demonstrates her/his expertise in the processes they use; their facilitation skills; and knowledge of resources the group can utilise to meet their aims.

What are the outcomes or desired results from the work?

Sometimes this work is referred to as 'sustainable' community work, meaning that the work has a chance of continuing on without the direct input of a worker. However, sustainability may not be the goal of every piece of work, as sometimes activities are time or project-specific. The view held by those working at the Nambour Community Centre is that a sustainable community is one that has strength, resilience and capacity to act. This includes the capacity of community members to tackle new or complex projects that meet their particular needs. Additionally, it includes strength and capacity to stand against oppressive processes or structures, which are encountered too often in community life. Therefore, community development is not just about community-building efforts, but also forms of community activism. The litmus test for sustainability is that those who have participated in various projects will have developed new skills; new community resources will have been acquired and perhaps, newly developed infrastructure that supports the various activities will have been established. In essence, sustainability means that people will have the skills, resources and connections with others to engage in a range of endeavours without a worker's involvement in the long-term.

The aim of the work is for people to be empowered and skilled up throughout the processes used, and to make connections with others. The results should be that participants are no longer isolated - they have each other; they have new skills and new information about ways in which they can solve problems in their own lives, either individually or collectively.

Finally, this work is about social change. It is not just reactive to social problems as they arise, but it is proactive, by looking at and addressing the root cause of issues. This means practitioners and community members can be working at two levels at the same time with the one issue. That is, working together with people affected by the issue to develop responses locally; and working at a social policy / social planning level to redress the situation or to prevent it from re-occurring. In this regard, the work is transformative as it seeks to create something new from the work. This might include new infrastructure, new resources or new outcomes, which benefit people in the long-term.

The relational method – from private concerns to public action

The '0-1-3' bonding and banding together

The 0-1-3 method begins with the idea that when we are alone there is no relationship (0) and any issues or concerns remain private, ours alone. With two people there is one (1) relationship, but the relationship still remains primarily within the realm of the personal, for each participant is central to the structure of the relationship. So, any issues or concerns remain private. With three people there are three (3) relationships and *shared* issues become public issues. The concern only becomes completely 'public' when there is a 'three-person' relationship, because no *one* can occupy all the relationships (Burkett, 2007).

Keep adding people into this equation, and the increase in the number of relationships is expediential e.g. four people = six different relationships, and so on. The benefit of being in relationship with two or more people is that if one person were to leave the relationship, then no one person would be alone. In the Sunshine Coast context that is known for having a very transient community, this relational method is helpful because it reduces social isolation experienced by many who live in the region. Social isolation is known to be one of the causal factors in depression and other detrimental health scenarios.

This common sense idea of banding together with others seems simple. As one practitioner put it, 'it's not rocket science'. However, thinking from the perspective of this as an approach to community development practice, the 0-1-3 becomes essential when we desire to work in the *public* realm as development workers, as opposed to the *private* realm in which most service delivery takes place. The 0-1-3 method builds relationships amongst people and creates groups by which public action can take place.

In the private realm, such as with counselling or casework, when the intervention is completed, no new relationships other than with the worker have necessarily been established. In the private realm however, this is not the aim; there are therapeutic or other aims driving these types of interventions. Further, there are therapeutic groups located in the public realm and in these, the worker often plays a 'coordinating' role and usually has expert knowledge about the subject matter that has brought the group together. For example, a post-natal depression support group led by a health worker, or a domestic violence therapeutic group with survivors of domestic violence, led by a domestic violence prevention worker. Another difference between these types of groups is that therapeutic groups aim for therapeutic outcomes and community development groups aim for public action, which builds social capital and enables groups of individuals to collectively create the kind of communities in which they wish to live, work and play. Having acknowledged this however, it has been said by people who have engaged in various community development projects and developed skills and friendships as a result, that the outcomes of their involvement felt very therapeutic. This is just not the aim.

A community development practitioner takes on the role of 'facilitator' as opposed to 'coordinator' when working with groups. In the beginning of group formation, practitioners are often the central hub of the group because they are likely to have a relationship with most of the group members, that is, they have done their 0-1's and bonded with individuals. The practitioner aims to move to the edge of the group, alongside all the other members, so that group members develop strong relationships with each other and begin to take responsibility for running the group themselves. This mechanism gives groups the greatest chance to be self-sustaining.

'0-1-3' - Stories from practice

Nambour Community Centre has engaged in a range of developmental projects in recent years. What follows are a few stories from our practice. The first two stories are from our multicultural community development program, facilitated by community development practitioner, Naomi Wiley. The third story is from our generalist community development program and the fourth is an organisational development story, in which I engaged in the development work in my role as community development worker and coordinator of the centre. All of these stories articulate how people have bonded and banded together to create social change on the Sunshine Coast.

The 'United in Diversity' and 'Srikandi – Indonesia' Groups

In 2005 a new community development program was established at the Nambour Community Centre. Naomi Wiley, the multicultural community worker set out to meet the broad aims of what became known as the 'Cultural Connections' program. The aims included: creating inclusive and sustainable culturally diverse communities on the Sunshine Coast; advancing multiculturalism; reducing the deleterious effects of racism, and providing opportunities for people from culturally and linguistically diverse (CALD) backgrounds to increase their citizenship within society. A two-pronged approach was used: to develop relationships with community members from CALD backgrounds and to develop relationships with service providers and the wider community.

Moving issues from private concern to public action began with Naomi hearing individual stories. For a period of a few months she went to many meetings, events, picnics, culturally specific gatherings and dinners. The outcomes associated with these processes are sometimes referred to as 'community engagement'. The purpose of this engagement was to hear the stories of those she met, listen for themes that emerged from the stories, ideas, and issues, and look for trends. Two clear themes emerged from these early connections. Firstly, *social isolation* associated with the process of migration and secondly, the need to create opportunities to *earn an income*. Many people were interested in various small business ideas and ventures.

To provide a response to the first theme – social isolation, the 0-1-3 method was used. Naomi asked people if they would like to connect with others who had similar ideas whom she had met in her new role. People came together and shared their stories of migration, their hopes and dreams, and their struggles of living in this country. The group members bonded quickly and they decided to keep meeting fortnightly. After a while, and because they had gained so much from the process, the group decided to put on a multicultural celebration with the hope of forming other connections and bringing other newly migrated people together. They took the opportunity to apply for a small grant to assist with the costs associated with hosting the event. The Nambour Community Centre auspiced their application for which they had to decide on a name for the group. They chose 'United in Diversity'. They were successful with their application and this meant that their informal group quickly shifted to a more semi-formal one, which now had responsibilities for financial accountability, deadlines to meet and much to organise to host the event.

The event attracted over 100 people and was hailed a great success. The women of United in Diversity gained a great sense of achievement, made many new connections and multiculturalism on the Sunshine Coast was celebrated. The United in Diversity group continues to meet, while acknowledging the natural ebb and flow of energy the members have depending on their life circumstances, a variety of different group activities has since taken place.

One of the spin-off activities from this original United in Diversity process was the establishment of the 'Srikandi – Indonesia Women's Group'. As this group conducts its meetings in Bahasa Indonesian, a member of United in Diversity took on a leadership role informing and facilitating the group. As Naomi does not speak this language her role is less about facilitation and more about support and resourcing. Naomi contributes to the group in a range of ways including building bridges to mainstream resources and the wider community. This dynamic group has continued to meet; its recent activities have included a feast to signify the end of Ramadan, and a seminar on women's rights. These events were open to the public and were, among other things, a great opportunity for members of the wider community to learn about and build bridges with Muslims on the Sunshine Coast.

In both the United in Diversity and Srikandi groups, through the 0-1-3 process, new connections have been facilitated that bring about a greater sense of community belonging for the members. Both groups needed to develop what are referred to as 'community analyses' about the collective needs of group members and how to respond to these needs. A community analysis is one in which group members develop a shared understanding of what is to be undertaken together; how they wish to work together; and they make a commitment to undertake the plans made.

The skills that members of United in Diversity have developed throughout this process have increased their individual capacity and confidence and the strategies for action they have employed collectively have meant that community capacity has been built. New infrastructure has been established by the formation of the Srikandi Indonesia Women's group. These two community development processes have taken place over a two-year period. This developmental approach to community building is slow. It is necessarily slow, to ensure all individuals become integral to the group processes, and therefore the pace must match the slowest participant. Working with community groups to bring about social change, is about taking a series of small strategic and intentional steps. The o-1-3 method employs a disciplined approach to making and sustaining connections with community members, and has a flow-on or 'ripple' effect in that skills are learned and applied to new situations and contexts by those who have participated.

Community education – small business skills with CALD participants

The second theme that emerged from engagement with community members - the need to earn an income, was responded to using a community education strategy. Naomi had also been connecting with established services on the Sunshine Coast to ascertain in what ways they might be utilised to bring about the aims of the Cultural Connections program. One of those services was a registered training organisation that had an interest in seeking funding for training small business skills with community members. A community education approach to assist individuals gain skills in establishing their own small businesses was undertaken. Using the o-1-3 method Naomi facilitated relationship development between people from CALD backgrounds, the registered training organisation, and people with small business experience from the wider community to provide a mentoring role with participants. Funding was obtained to teach a twelve-week course on small business skills and Naomi, utilising her expertise in cross-cultural communication, was able to assist the training organisation to deliver the learning modules in ways in which participants would most benefit. A small group of participants from the course continue to meet to provide peer support and peer mentoring in their business endeavours. Naomi continues to create bridges between participants and state and local government programs that assist small business owners and sole traders establish their businesses.

Multiple starting points – traversing the developmental continuum

The Nambour Community Centre is one of over one hundred neighbourhood centres funded in Queensland by the State Government's Department of Communities. Like many of this cohort, the Nambour Community Centre has over the years succumbed to neo-liberal influences, and operated its programs only within a service delivery paradigm. However, the beauty of the developmental method and its influence on social services work comes with the knowledge that there is always a more developmental way of doing a particular piece of work. Traditional service delivery can be moved along a 'developmental continuum'. This is where work is conducted in the same general area of community need, but from a bottom-up approach where the people involved determine the processes and outcomes of the work.

One process used at the Nambour Community Centre to drive an existing piece of work along the developmental continuum, occurred with an existing budget counselling service for individuals. This activity was part of an anti-poverty strategy and was located in the private realm of service delivery. The question was asked, 'How can we locate this activity within the public realm?' This individual-focused work was moved into a collective process by conducting a six-week budgeting course with a group of individuals. The course was called, 'Living Well on Less'. The workers took an educative stance, where participants themselves did most of the educating, not the workers facilitating the course. This approach to community education articulated by Paulo Freire (1970) is where we join our content or knowledge with the knowledge and lived experience of participants, and together move forward in action. This approach is very different to regular community education where normally the teacher is the expert imparting specific knowledge on a particular subject matter. With Living Well on Less, the facilitators knew that the participants who were already living on fixed low incomes were best placed to share their ideas about how to survive and thrive personally in these situations. The collective wisdom of the group was powerful.

From this community education activity, a savings and loans circle was established. Savings and loans circles are money cooperatives, where individuals come together regularly and pool small sums of their money into a common fund. Members then borrow from the common pool with a no-interest loan for items that the group has approved. The individual loans are paid back over a two-year period, whilst members continue to add to the common fund with their monthly contributions. The 'SOS Savings and Loans Club' is a group formation activity, which has had a long-term, sustainable approach to reducing the effects of poverty for people living on the Sunshine Coast.

A commitment to shift a piece of work from service delivery to community development usually involves the practitioner taking an educative stance with participants, other workers, members of their governing body and funding bodies. However, in the long run, self-sustaining groups allow a practitioner to move on to new community activities, as the confidence and skills of participants develop. Therefore, in the long run this approach is an effective one and also creates efficiencies as community members continue working on projects with newfound skills themselves. Utilising the 0-1-3 method this shift in practice from individual budget counselling, to community education group work, and then to the formation of a co-operative is an example of how a piece of work organically evolved. This developmental work met the Centre's general aim of reducing the effects of poverty, and was driven by and achieved by the people themselves.

Developmental community work at the macro & meta levels – the Sunshine Coast Community Co-operative Ltd

The same principles and approaches to community development work at a grass roots level can also be applied at macro, sector, or organisational development levels. In May 2007 the Sunshine Coast Community Co-operative Ltd was registered with the Office of Fair Trading as a non-trading co-operative. This had been the culmination of almost two years work to establish a regional community development entity on the Sunshine Coast. The formation members of the co-op are: the Maroochy Neighbourhood Centre, the Nambour Community Centre, the Caloundra Community Centre and the Hinterland Community Development Association of Caloundra. These four organisations are separate incorporated associations, each working in different locations on the Sunshine Coast.

This entity was formed because of the contemporary forces impacting on the four organisations. During the late 1980s and early 1990s, neo-liberal political ideology brought about substantial change in the way funded community services were conducted. To some extent, these changes saw services shift from humanitarian ideals to those driven by both 'managerialist' and 'marketised' discourses. Economic rationalism and managerialism, which is seeing market logic applied to community services, place emphasis on short-term measurable outcomes of service delivery. This has affected the way practitioners engage in funded community development and other social service program work.

On the Sunshine Coast the trend for social service organisations to adapt to the current context has seen organisations respond in a number of ways. These include: growing their businesses; changing their legal entity status to 'company limited by guarantee' to establish a 'for-profit' arm; amalgamating with smaller organisations; and increasing the scope of their work to new geographic and social service provision areas. This is all being done so organisations can become competitive and relevant in this contemporary context.

The four organisations involved in the Sunshine Coast Community Co-op however, did not want to amalgamate and run the risk of losing their local, grass-roots approach to the community work they currently have and which they do very well. Nor did they want to succumb to the dominant paradigm of competition. So, with a history of working informally together, and because they had developed a shared or community analysis, the four management committees and senior workers of the organisations foresaw the wonderful benefits of banding together and formally partnering, whilst remaining independent organisations. The Sunshine Coast Community Co-op is working together in a number of ways to partner on both operational and governance-related activities, which they believe will benefit themselves as individual organisations and also have flow-on benefits for the community members with whom they work across the Sunshine Coast.

Conclusion

The method referred to in this chapter has a rich history, steeped in tradition and revolutionary ideals. It relies on tenets such as mutuality and reciprocity. However, community development practitioners come across all sorts of people in the course of their work and developmental community work falls on the self-help side of social services work. Therefore, it should be noted that not all community members are ready for this developmental approach. Some people may need individual support through counselling, or other service delivery to help them deal with the adversity they have experienced or are experiencing in their lives. People need to be ready to take control of their lives and environments, and they need to want to do this in the public realm in which community development occurs. For those who are not at this place, other forms of social services work may be more appropriate, and referrals to agencies that can help are often required.

For the many people who are ready for this developmental approach, these methods to community building offer empowering and sustainable outcomes as well as pathways for effective citizenship. Community development practitioners need to be prepared to approach the work as the learner, not the expert; they need to be a facilitator, not the coordinator or driver; they need to carry their agenda lightly; and they need to go at the pace of the community, or the slowest amongst the group to ensure *all* are integral to the process. By doing so, by situating themselves alongside individuals, groups and communities and engaging *with* them in their struggles, a true journey of mutuality and shared responsibility to meet need will be facilitated. It is imperative that workers do not view those they work with as 'the other', where differences are objectified, but rather acknowledge togetherness in the face of their shared humanity. This is how a truly civil society is created and celebrated.

References

Andrews, D. (2004). Vocational professionals. *Praxis. 1,* 18-28.
Bhattacharyya, J. (2004). Theorizing community development. *Journal of the Community Development Society. 34*(2), 5-23.
Buber, M. (1937). *I and thou.* New York: Charles Scribner's Sons.
[Burkett, I.] (2007). "Note from Editor" in Lathouras, T. The Srikandhi and United in Diversity Groups: A story of community development from Nambour, Queensland. Newsletter of the *International Association for Community Development*, Oceania Special Issue, August 2007.
Dasgupta, S. (1974). *Problems with peace research – A third world view.* New Delhi: Indian Council of Peace Research.
Kelly, A. (2005). *Flirting with spirituality, re-enchanting community* – The Les Halliwell Address, 2005 CD Queensland Community Development Conference, Maleny, Australia.
Kelly, A. (2008). *Development method – Workbook.* Brisbane: The Centre for Social Response.
Kelly, A. & Sewell, S. (1988). *With head, heart and hand.* Brisbane: Boolarong Press.
Westoby, P. & Owen, J. R. (2009). The sociality and geometry of community development practice. *Community Development Journal* [advanced access online: o: bsp005v], 1 – 17.

Chapter 3
The Circle of Men Project

A Story of Tackling Social Isolation in Men Who Live in Aged Care Facilities in Redlands

Ross Wiseman

As a teacher in community development, I engage myself in various community organisations and projects both to express my own desire for social change and to identify suitable real life community projects and tasks for my students. The Redlands District Committee of the Ageing (RDCOTA) is one such involvement.

Through this involvement I participated in meetings to address the high rate of suicide in older men. This is where I first met Mike and Washuntara, two community members I have come to greatly respect. This chapter is about their story of reaching out to older men in an aged care facility in the Redland Shire. They became frustrated that those concerned about suicide in Redlands were not reaching out and listening to the personal concerns of older men themselves. Mike and Washuntara initiated a Circle of Men, by setting up a weekly gathering with a group of men in one of the privately operated residential facilities in the Redlands. In 2006, I was invited to attend one of these meetings and it sparked in me a passion to continue supporting Mike and Washuntara in their venture.

Mike and Washuntara set out to build connections to older men who were likely to be experiencing the deep sense of social isolation often identified in aged care facilities. It has been said that the four enemies that face older people, particularly those in aged care facilities, are boredom, loneliness, depression and helplessness. Hopelessness could well be added to this litany. The story takes place within the wider context of current social policy through which aged care facilities, whether operated through for-profit or not-for-profit organisations, are rarely funded and staffed in ways that sufficiently foster the social and emotional well being of residents. As Mike and Washuntara encountered this first hand, they became increasingly distressed, angry and determined. They began to recognise the enormity of the issue and they sought help from RDCOTA and others to address the situation. The first part of this chapter tells the story of Mike and Washuntara engaging with older men. The second part puts this story in the context of social and political changes of the time. The third part brings the story up to the present moment when Mike and Washuntara, along with RDCOTA are considering how to provide structural support and stability so the project is sustainable.

Part One: The Circle of Men Project

Frank and Smith (1999) explain that although conditions that warrant a community development initiative may exist within a community, a catalyst is needed to activate change within that community. A catalyst may emerge in the form of a person, an event, or maybe even a planned situation. But it is a person or people who typically create a vision of what is possible. These people are the ones who take the first steps to bring about change through community development methods.

Mike, who retired some years ago, claims he has nothing of significance in his background that prepared him for his work as a catalyst with the older male residents in the aged care facility. He happened upon this cause more by chance in his search for meaningful and effective work in his retirement. Attending the meetings about suicide left him frustrated and this stirred him into action. Mike has a strong natural insight into human behaviour, a strong sense of social justice, and a commitment to empowerment of individuals. He has a quiet demeanour and considered speech, but he has a well developed ability to organise and network, and he concedes that he has a personal hunger for achieving deeper levels of male friendship in his life.

Washuntara, more than twenty years Mike's junior, is an accomplished professional singer and songwriter. He lived for many years in the USA where he was influenced by the men's movement and where he worked with a range of social issues and people, including senior citizens and men's groups. With his performing arts background and his 'free spirit', he has a formidable set of group facilitation skills and empathy. Washuntara told me that he approached the men's suicide group as a natural extension of his lengthy community involvement with men. He grew up in a family where men related strongly with each other and he was influenced by his relations with these men. He feels men are losing their way, getting too involved in high stress lifestyles and not relating enough to each other and family. He shares Mike's insight and strong sense of social justice and empowerment. However, he is the entertainer, the extrovert and the natural democratic leader.

The impetus for Mike and Washuntara getting together was an announcement at a community meeting that a local aged care facility had requested some men to come along and engage with men who were lonely. At that meeting, no one showed interest, but later Mike and Washuntara discussed it, and decided to take up the opportunity. They went off to the facility and talked with the Director of Nursing. Keen to have some volunteers, she responded immediately and the agreement was struck that Mike and Washuntara would meet on a weekly basis with all of the men who lived there.

At their first meeting, staff had organised some of the men to attend on the basis that some volunteers were visiting. An afternoon tea had been arranged. They had a general chat. Mike says: 'it developed from that'. Knowing Mike, he used a range of skills to put people at ease, settle them, and encourage them to share something of themselves in the group. The question 'What is it like living here?' opened up discussion. Music, humour, self-disclosure, some funny stories, helped the process. The men agreed to continue meeting each Monday afternoon.

Mike and Washuntara found it significant that the men they met with, all living in the same facility, were actually strangers to each other. They wondered how this could be.

The formula for the gatherings developed in response to the men's interests and concerns. It included afternoon tea and spending some of the time with Washuntara lifting everyone's spirits with his guitar and the piano, and his singing and banter. Mike and Washuntara hoped this would build the relationships and assist the men to listen to each others stories, share concerns and discuss problems they were experiencing. Mike and Washuntara talked to me of their hopes of it developing into a mutual support group. In community development terms I saw this as a hope that the group would become meaningful to the men, that they would develop a sense of ownership, and that some of their private issues would emerge as shared concerns to be addressed together.

Over time, the men became more forward in expressing what they wished to accomplish through the group. This began when the men started to share the kinds of things they missed and would love to do, like visiting a pub or getting out into the community. Knowing how to respond collectively to their various individual needs has sometimes been challenging. Mike says that in many respects the men are not a group, in the sense that 'they do not share a unified theme'. Mike and Washuntara had to learn to 'start where each of the men is at'. They identify activities that suit individual needs and wishes, then encouraging others to join in and participate, with the result that some do enthusiastically, and others less so. The occasional conflict in whose needs should be met, and how, is usually managed through encouraging overall participation ensuring that over time, every-one gets the chance to say what the group will do.

Outings away from the aged care facility have become quite popular for the majority, but not for others, and a challenging feat for some. In the eighteen months the group has been operating, they have visited clubs on the Bay Islands for barbecues; had trips up the length of the Brisbane River on the city-cat ferries; and had lunch outings at popular pubs or at clubs on the Bay Islands and the like.

On the first city-cat trip, one of the men who had worked for decades in Brisbane's central business district was visibly moved to tears, as he never believed he would see the city skyline again. Mike likes to talk of the time Washuntara introduced the group of men to the ferry staff as a group of re-tired doctors, and enjoyed watching the marked change in the attitudes and responses of the staff.

Transport for outings remains a concern. Having the required number of maxi-taxis turn up at the same time is difficult which creates further trouble in maintaining firm protocols with the taxi company. Another is-sue is having sufficient suitable volunteers to assist the more frail men, and those in wheel chairs. Another is ensuring that all activities are totally covered by insurance. Mike says that they have been able to attract differ-ent individuals as helper volunteers at times, but retaining their commit-ment is difficult. The men do enjoy having different company. Classes of TAFE students have often visited the meetings and gone on boat trips with the men. The students are particularly popular with the men because they are mostly younger women. Conversely, this intimate contact with the older men typically has a profound impact on younger students. The ex-perience opens up their own feelings about relations with male members of their family, especially where sadness, loss or unresolved issues have exis-ted. Seeing students so visibly moved by these contacts confirms for me the value of Mike and Washuntara's belief in the importance of intergenera-tional relationships.

Mike and Washuntara maintain direction through the idea that their role is about 'breaking down the walls' that separate the men and the com-munity. They try to bring the outside community into the world of the men in the facility, and take the men out into the community – both regu-larly and consistently, and on their own terms.

Communication between group members when they meet can be quite challenging. A number of the men have quite serious hearing loss. Others suffer the effects of medication or dementia. Mike is determined that they continue to find solutions both through communicating effectively and en-suring people have the technological aids they need.

The men say they feel the female staff tend to be patronising towards them. Washuntara interprets this as about the predominance of women and the prevailing female culture of the establishment. Female residents outnumber the men by something in the order of 9 to 1 and almost the en-tire staff cohort is female. It is difficult to disentangle the various threads surrounding this issue, with gender and culture both impacting the kinds of roles and relationships both staff and residents assume in order to survive institutional life. What the men find, however, is that the opportunity to talk about their experience of these things with other men is important to them.

Mike's view is that it is important to acknowledge the key roles the men previously held, such as fathers, teachers, managers, and skilled workmen. It is also important to acknowledge the sense of loss as those roles recede and one becomes more dependent. Mike says that by the time men have been admitted to an aged care facility, their self-esteem and communication skills may be in decline. They have lost their partners and dear friends, lost the roles they have relied upon for their self-esteem and personal support. They may be less likely to assert their needs in an alien environment through concern that complaints might be interpreted as trouble making. So they are likely to suffer in silence. Institutionalisation magnifies the feelings of helplessness and lost dignity which are common in older age.

Several members of the Circle of Men have passed away in the period since Mike and Washuntara commenced. The men discussed their concern that no one in the group is informed when this occurs. Someone may be missing, the men feel alarmed, but no one tells them what is happening. Staff say that privacy legislation governs who can be informed at the time. It is often on a Monday, in the group, that news of a death is heard about. The men can share their feelings and responses to these events and to make appropriate observances. On a number of occasions, the Monday group has been a catalyst for gathering a party of the men, with Mike and Washuntara, to attend the funeral. Observances and rituals are as, if not more, important to this group of people as anyone else in the community. Death is a significant theme for older people, especially in a nursing home, and the feelings that are raised need to be acknowledged and addressed for all residents.

After eighteen months of the Circle of Men, however, Mike says that there definitely have been shifts. The men now know each other, and share the problems that they are each sorting through. They are decidedly more happy and willing to discuss their issues in the group, and are less inclined to seek out one-on-one situations. They outwardly demonstrate more warmth and concern towards each other. Quite a number of them actively seek a hug or other body contact when meeting each week.

One key disappointment is that despite the bonding and camaraderie developed in the group, the men do not seek each other out beyond the Monday sessions. Mike and Washuntara have suggested to the men that they spend time with each other socially and for support, as well as socialising over meal times. However this suggestion meets with no success. Some of the men have explained that this is because as they seldom go out, there is little new that happens in their lives to talk about. They would only be telling each other the stories or news that they already knew. Mike and Washuntara think it may be difficult for the men to reach out to each other, when the issues are so close to home. They all struggle with loneliness, depression, hopelessness and helplessness, or fear of death. This is hard for men in general, and particularly so for the men of the present older generation who lived through world wars, and learned to suppress complex feelings. The men say they prefer to meet when Mike and Washuntara are there to lighten the load.

When the men have concerns about things that are happening or not happening in the facility, Mike says that they encourage them to express such concerns to staff. Sometimes, with the men's permission, Mike and Washuntara have discussed concerns with staff and asked them to follow up. However, the follow up never seems to happen. Both nursing staff and diversional therapists have noticed the benefits from the group, but they have not tried to build upon, or translate this, to other facility operations. The staff rarely prepared the men for the regular Circle of Men meetings; they have rarely supported and encouraged the men to attend when they are not feeling motivated; and they have rarely provided the physical support in getting the men to the meeting room. The men are not always ready or motivated to attend, so Mike and Washuntara often take the time to offer them support and encouragement, after which the men typically make the effort and subsequently appreciate it and say so.

Mike and Washuntara have discussed their concerns with the manager of the facility. She agrees with their analysis of what should or could be happening, but says that there is simply not the staff nor the resources for staff to do any more than they are presently able. She says staff envies the time Mike and Washuntara spend with the men, but feel guilty themselves if they sit down and talk and ignore other tasks. There is an important dialogue happening here between Mike and Washuntara and the manager, but at this point there is no significant change.

A key strength for Mike and Washuntara has been to keep in mind their initial impetus that was to bring the outside in and take the inside out. When they were asked by management of another facility to come and visit their residents, Mike and Washuntara negotiated that residents from the two facilities visit each other. This has created multiple benefits, with groups having an outing or having visitors, resulting in more social interaction and the two facilities becoming more open to the world outside.

Mike and Washuntara are firm in their adherence to a flexible developmental approach where the individual needs of each resident are openly and regularly reviewed and built into a changing range of activities mutually agreed upon within the group, but always including the time and encouragement for men to share what is occurring with them internally or externally. This approach respects the individuality of each man, whilst continuing to build the relationships between men and their sense of being part of a collective.

It may not be possible for a structured facility with all the constraints of organisational and financial management to be as responsive as Mike and Washuntara would wish. Yet, nor is it possible for them to reach all the older residents in aged care facilities in their own local area, let alone further afield. In my most recent discussions with Mike and Washuntara, the focus has repeatedly returned to two key challenges. Firstly, what all this means for those of us who want people everywhere to be respected and treated with dignity in the face of a burgeoning aged care industry which despite the rhetoric and all the quality assurance processes, is not yet able to achieve this, nor likely to. Secondly, how to structure, sustain and build on the current work and directions of the Circle of Men. In the next sections, each of these is discussed, beginning with a social analysis.

Part Two: Social Analysis and Context

Mike and Washuntara's story is about a small local activity embedded within multiple layers of social, economic and political practice. In this section we look at how local issues raised in the story are shaped by broader aged care policy and the specific application of this in Redland Shire. In community development terms this is about connecting the private experience of people to the public world of structures, policy and planning.

The story raises issues about loneliness and social isolation particularly in male residents of aged care facilities. It raises issues of how our society cares for older people and the translation of this into aged care as an industry. It raises issues of resourcing and how institutional resources are prioritised. It raises issues of the adequacy of privatised, managerial and business models as a means of providing care for older people. It raises issues of the practices (and training) of staff in aged care institutions and it raises issues about the values and beliefs of the broader community.

Aged care policy

Some years ago governments recognised that the future demographics of ageing would place a significant economic and social burden on the working population unless shifts in policy occurred. Resulting shifts have largely been in the direction of what is termed 'ageing in place' (or staying at home) with a level of community-based support. This is now widely viewed as the preferred future for the majority of older people. Institutional care has become significantly privatised, with increasing numbers of for-profit providers entering what is now commonly referred to as the 'market'. Government responsibility is exercised via: funding for individuals entering aged care institutions; provision of in-home packages and services; and monitoring of standards in terms of quality and compliance.

Commonwealth aged care standards make provision for personal, civic, legal and consumer rights, ideally enabling the individual to retain active control over their lives whether within residential care or private home environs. The resident's emotional wellbeing is considered with emphasis on supporting adjustment to communal living and coping with grief and loss. Independence is valued, with individual preferences catered for and community involvement and family networks encouraged. Emphasis is placed on leisure activities indicating individual preference with family and community involvement. However, whilst these standards may be ideally sound, a lack of compliance by service providers and practitioners is only identified via complaint or audit (Dept of Health and Ageing, 2003) begging the question of how well these ideal standards are actually met in the everyday lives of older people residing in aged care facilities. For example, Standard 3.5 states that

residents are assisted to achieve maximum independence, maintain
friendships and participate in the life of the community, within and
outside the residential care service

and

strategies to maximise community involvement are reviewed
regularly with residents, their families and community members

(Dept of Health and Ageing, 2004).

However, with accreditation of aged care facilities generally conducted in three year cycles (largely self-assessed) (Dept of Health and Ageing, 2003) and otherwise relying on resident or advocate complaint, it is questionable as to how well the achievement of such standards may be effectively observed, monitored and enforced.

Community attitudes and beliefs

As Ife (2002) suggests, community analyses will vary. In response to there being gaps in addressing any important social needs, there will be people who, legitimately or otherwise, blame the individual, the rescuer, the system or the discourse, and each begins their analysis and action to address the issue based in their particular belief. The task in community development is often one of working with the diverse groups to develop a shared analysis and understanding of needs and rights. This requires seeing from the various perspectives and always requires that the least powerful people are included.

Washuntara's analysis came largely from a gender perspective, concerning men's social conditioning, and also a leftist analysis in which he was inclined to blame the private providers of the residential facilities (the capitalists out to make a profit). Mike on the other hand came with a business background and was more inclined to view providers as having a job to do, but experiencing resourcing constraints. Mike saw a valuable role for volunteers within the whole picture, and also saw the added value that keeping the community involved could provide.

A diverse range of wider community views arise from the issues embedded within this story. These include the views that such problems are caused through the cultural maladjustment of males within the broader Australian cultural context, or that they are the result of the typical institutional environment that is inherent within aged care settings, giving rise to the condition of 'institutionalisation' (Goffmann, 1959; Goffmann, 1962).

There is also a view that the problems arise out of the broader changes that have occurred within our society, our families, our industries, our government and political structures, which tend to socialise people into systems where they are dealt with either as empowered survivors or disempowered welfare cases. Then there is the view that the problems arise out of a combination of all of these factors. Whichever the case, a chicken and egg question arises as to whether it is these broader societal and cultural attitudes that drive government policy to create systems that produce social isolation, or whether these broader attitudes are formed as a result of government policy.

I have engaged in many discussions with Mike and Washuntara and with others in the broader Redlands networks about the situation, with each interchange being underpinned by the basic analysis that whilst there is a valuable role for community it must also be acknowledged that aged care funding must be adequate and providers must meet the standards established by the government on the community's behalf. While occupational health and safety provisions require the building of walls around residential care facilities, it is vitally important that these walls do not become a barrier to engagement between people inside and people outside. If the community abandons people to life within the walls, that life will become diminished in many ways. If, however, community members maintain active engagement, then a form of awareness raising ('conscientisation' in Friere's, 1973 terms) will happen and the community will want to ensure that the care that happens is the kind of care they would want for themselves.

Several community attitudes operate against this level of engagement. People assume families will take the main responsibility for visiting and maintaining residents' emotional and social lives. It may also be that denial of old age and death is a barrier that keeps younger community members away. In other words, there is an unspoken community interest in shutting older people away, out of sight (de Beauvoir, 1972). For me then, action by many people each acting from their own understanding of the situation, will all produce some benefits in opening up the situation and indicating the changes that are needed. Yet, it is also necessary that we keep scanning the bigger picture and that we have some structures at a community level which make it their business to speak with, and on behalf of, the most vulnerable people, whilst also keeping all the players within a dialogue of change.

Staffing and practices

A significant point of distress for the Circle of Men has been that staff practices are often routinised to the point that residents lose touch with their own unique selfhood and dignity. There are not enough hours in the day, or staff to do the jobs, to provide the personalised engagement that we all need to experience in the place we call home. The multiple and demanding roles of aged care staff (physical care, medical care, hygiene, mobility and the like) may mean there are too many expectations for meeting intimacy needs of residents, particularly if staff are in short supply. At the point of life where we are losing so much, there are so few opportunities to have this recognised and satisfied.

Lack of intimacy may be a key to the social isolation (boredom, loneliness, depression, helplessness and hopelessness) people feel. The constant reminder of one's own impending mortality prevails in residents of aged care facilities. Human contact itself is not the entire solution, but a certain depth of human contact may well be.

Is it reasonable to ask of staff that they take the time to engage with each resident in a way that acknowledges them and touches their inner life? If it is a fair ask, then institutional resources need to be made available. If it is a fair ask, is education and training adequate to prepare staff so that they understand different levels and modes of communication and can communicate with ease at an intimate level about a resident's innermost feelings and experiences? Given the likely extent of social isolation among residents in aged care facilities, in this case male residents, it is proposed that staff would need to be highly proficient in developing and maintaining high quality relationships with numerous residents almost as a matter of course. Whether this is essentially a question about adequate time or adequate training or about prevailing staff culture, or even about quality industry standards or their implementation, is a moot point. Enhancing the care of older people means addressing all of these factors.

A key role in aged care is that of the Diversional Therapist (DT) or Diversion Therapist Assistant (DTA). This is a demanding role caught between the needs people have for relationship, intimacy and care and the institutional necessities for a planned, structured and advertised program of activities. No matter how good the consultations and resident's committees, the lived experience of the individual may be one of being done to and managed rather than related with. Mike and Washuntara view community input to be a vital complement to what Diversional Therapists offer. Community relationships can touch many aspects of life, with activities and outings being only one component. Out of wide ranging discussions, the men would be enabled to articulate what *they* like to do and participate meaningfully in the planning. The quality and depth of relationships, however, become the motivating factor because they promise recognition of the individual, a genuine experience of life, engagement, camaraderie and fun.

Mike believes that pre-prepared programs of activity within facilities provide simulated experience, and he is keen that people from the community engage personally around genuine experiences. Both Mike and Washuntara remain firmly committed to a flexible developmental approach where the individual needs of each resident are openly and regularly reviewed and built into a changing range of activities mutually agreed upon within the group, but always including the time and encouragement for men to share what is occurring with them internally or externally. The particular approach preferred by Mike and Washuntara may well make the whole process rather too unpredictable for the systems of a bureaucratically programmed and structured organisation. This then raises the matter of staff management systems and the operation and ownership of aged care facilities.

It is not difficult to locate facts and views about problems that are widespread within the staffing and operation of aged care facilities throughout Australia and throughout most western democracies. The sustainability of quality residential care is significantly threatened as a result of the shift to aged care facilities being increasingly contracted to for-profit corporate organisations emphasising business and managerial models of service delivery (O'Rielly, Courtney and Edwards, 2007). Foremost among these issues is the comprehensive contradiction and failure of a competitive market-based system to deliver quality residential aged care while maximising profits for owners and shareholders.

Aside from such fundamental flaws contained within a market-based system, a further critical factor for consideration is the industrial conditions under which staff is employed. As outlined by the Australian Nursing Federation (2004) and Venturato, Kellet and Windsor (2007) the shift to a market-based system has facilitated a lack of adequate government monitoring and regulation over the industry which has consequently resulted in:
- nursing and other staff deserting deteriorating working conditions within aged care facilities
- fear in remaining qualified staff of being held accountable for poor care caused by deteriorating standards
- increasing use of unqualified staff to assume greater responsibility than their qualifications warrant
- failure to adequately guarantee the rights of residents for quality care
- breaking down of the entire residential caring system
- a need to resort to more costly agency-based nursing care for bailing out a failing system.

Responsibility for change?

Australians have witnessed, and continue to witness, many such public failures of care in residential aged care agencies over the last decade. Given the increasing numbers of senior citizens who either live or have lived or are preparing to live in aged care facilities in this era, it can be presumed that there would be few in the community who have not had some contact with these facilities. Therefore, the first question to arise is, what are the perceptions held within the wider community about these institutions? Indeed advertising tends to euphemistically represent them as havens for the elderly, but what general knowledge does the community have of the issues that have been raised here? What knowledge does the community ignore? What explains why the community might not want to know, or not want to care? What needs to change to ensure that the wider community is more aware of the circumstances of residents in aged care facilities? What responsibility does the wider community have for aged care residents and the underlying factors that give rise to circumstances such as those raised? To what degree are the answers to these questions fashioned by prevailing social forces?

Finally, to what degree is the plight of male residents in aged care facilities a product of a male culture which has evolved over many decades and been punctuated by significant events such as the two World Wars and the Great Depression? To what degree has this culture created an inability in men to relate to themselves and to other men, particularly at the time in their lives when their personal support needs may be greatest and their capacity to assume responsibility for managing their own affairs the most limited? More importantly, how much has the present culture of younger men and boys changed so that they are better able to support themselves and each other?

Context: Redland Shire

Redland City is one of a number of local authority areas associated with the 'sea-change phenomenon' in Queensland that has adopted the growing industry of aged care and retirement villages as a major source of economic and employment activity. Once a prosperous area renowned for its strawberries, carnations and market gardens, which have all given way to housing developments, the city needed a replacement for its historical economic base of small crops and horticulture. As a result, commercial interests now strongly promote the area as the ideal place for retirement for those with self-funded superannuation savings.

There are now 21 retirement villages (or hostels) in the city, seven of which also serve as aged care facilities (low and high care). There are a further six facilities that are sole providers of aged care (low and high care). A number of additional retirement villages and aged care facilities are currently planned or under construction, some with hundreds of units. Consequently, there is a matching growth rate in the projected population of senior citizens in the city. For example, by 2016, the number of people aged 55 years and older living in Redlands is expected to increase by 58%, with some zones expecting increases from 142% to 185%. It is clear that this changing demography will place particular stress on aged care infrastructure, and on the resources of the wider community.

The City Council has already identified the needs of senior citizens as a top priority with the adoption of its 'Ageing Well in the Redlands Strategy' (2006). It has established the Redlands Advisory Group on Seniors Issues (RAGOSI), a group of local people to advise the Council and to assist in guiding the implementation of council strategy. The research supporting this strategy has already identified and prioritised social isolation of older people as a key issue requiring resource provision. However, while concerns about social isolation in aged care facilities are constantly raised within emerging aged care networks, this is not an area that comes within council responsibility. Instead, while building standards may be well developed and monitored, neither RAGOSI nor council has a voice in relation to the social and emotional well being of aged care facility residents.

Part Three: Infrastructure: Fork in the Road

Mike and Washuntara have a passion to see the Circle of Men grow and reach into more aged care facilities. Ideally, they would like to see it develop into a movement that has the capacity to change the provision of aged care in Australia. Such big dreams need a public structure to carry them forward. In community development terms, such global aspirations are approached via the linking up of many small local structures. At this point, Mike and Washuntara invited RDCOTA to assist them to think through some of the issues around structure and governance.

RDCOTA was at that time in the process of restructuring itself to better respond to the growth of aged care issues in Redlands. Mike and Washuntara's invitation raised many questions for the organisation to consider. What would its role be in supporting small and local community development initiatives? Should it auspice initiatives like that of Mike's and Washuntara's? Should it put timeframes and limits on its auspice role? Should it encourage such small groups to incorporate themselves or should it provide a long-term umbrella structure for community activity? These are very challenging issues for committee members who may have no background or training in community development, to get their heads around. The implications of the different options for management and staff time, legalities, insurances, resources and public relations, are significant.

The Circle of Men has a vision of itself as a movement, which in the immediate term aims to provide friendship between men in the community and men in aged care facilities, and in the medium term to challenge and address some of the problems emerging in aged care, and in the longer term to bring about change in both community attitudes towards ageing and in men about their social conditioning and relationships. However, there has been little evidence of men responding to this. So the Circle of Men is asking RDCOTA for help. As discussions have progressed it has become evident there is a fork in the road, which is explained below.

The fork in the road for the Circle of Men is whether to try and grow as a social movement or to formalise as a volunteer service. A social movement is by its nature unincorporated and informal and emphasises horizontal relationships between people. Service organisations by contrast establish vertical relationships between roles as a means of achieving objectives. The goals of women and men's movements for example have been to bring about social change and liberation from outmoded social conditioning. Within a movement, however, there may be formal organisations that exist to pursue more limited objectives (for example women's refuges within the women's movement). Yet attempts to incorporate horizontal processes such as collectives within organisations have proven very diffi-cult. The Circle of Men could possibly grow as a widening circle of hori-zontal relationships between men. The leadership would need to be intern-al to the circle. It would be difficult to achieve the insurance, legislative, financial and organisational arrangements associated with good contem-porary governance in such a model. It is possible that the Circle of Men could grow as a movement by men who are part of the circle volunteering as individuals to Aged care Facilities, with the facilities providing the insur-ances and legal support. In this model the Circle of Men would be the sup-port and mentoring group that provides the base from which men, as indi-viduals, go out to nursing homes. It is difficult to know how RDCOTA could resource such a model, except perhaps by assisting with articulation of the model and skills development to operate it. This could include some kind of manual to assist men to carry forward the Circle of Men philosophy and approach.

An alternative model, the other fork, is articulated by Karen Finlay (Redland City Council) and requires the Circle of Men to establish conven-tional governance processes. In this model the Circle of Men could incor-porate or be auspiced by RDCOTA, and in either case RDCOTA would assist in the identification of tasks and with management expertise. This would result in a volunteer program complete with tasks like recruitment and vetting of volunteers, establishing blue cards, providing insurances and legal frameworks and supervision.

The processes and outcomes of these two approaches will be quite different.

For RDCOTA, there is a different fork in the road. One possibility is for RDCOTA to support, with worker input, the growing up of the Circle of Men. This is a somewhat risky approach, as the Circle of Men is by nature an open process, not subjected to governance, vetting of recruits or formal role descriptions. If something went wrong in a nursing home, for example, because of an unvetted recruit, the RDCOTA responsibility would be legally and ethically unclear. Governance arrangements are im-portant precisely to clarify areas of responsibility. If the arrangements with aged care facilities were clearly negotiated, and if the Circle of Men engaged in good mentoring and support however, RDCOTA could negoti-ate a role of providing developmental support for a period of time.

Other options for RDCOTA may be to provide the umbrella of its own legislative structure, insurances and some financial support within a con-ventional auspicing structure. This would mean that the Circle of Men would be a self-governing structure within some minimal legal and insur-ance requirements. Some worker hours for developmental activities could be added in to this model.

At the other end of the spectrum, RDCOTA could establish within its own structure a volunteer program in which the Circle of Men sits. RDCOTA already has another resident-initiated project that involves vo-lunteers going into aged care facilities to engage people in structured activ-ities. These two projects could become part of a RDCOTA portfolio in which the recruitment, training, support and mentoring of volunteers to enhance life in aged care facilities is undertaken as a RDCOTA commitment. This of course, has implications in terms of the level of control that rests with Mike and Washuntara as the initiators of the Circle of Men.

Kelly and Sewell (1988) provide a compass for thinking through the implications of such decisions. The compass asks whose agenda, whose values, whose voices drive decision-making? Does the direction of change strengthen the horizontal (people's relations to each other in the community) or the vertical (the formal structures of the community or society) or are these genuinely reconciled to each other through dialogue and planning? Power is embedded within all these negotiations and, for Kelly and Sewell, the task is to ensure that the power of the vertical system does not neutralise or usurp the power of the horizontal.

At the point of writing, dialogue is ongoing. Mike and Washuntara are trying to work out what is best for the Circle of Men. RDCOTA is having many discussions, internally and with Mike and Washuntara. Community representatives are invited to have input as are the Association of Residential Care Providers, Volunteering Queensland and other friends of RDCOTA and the Circle of Men.

Evolving the model

First and foremost, Mike and Washuntara want to continue and improve what they have accomplished so far in this one facility. To achieve this, a range of issues needs to be tackled, the most important of which is additional community support to ensure the project's continuity. Their idea is that two small groups of male volunteers are needed. One group would take responsibility for the more practical tasks such as arranging a visiting program, assisting with mobility, participating in the meeting and tending to the residents' needs generally. A second smaller group would be trained to take on group facilitation and leadership roles in the life of the group. This would create a back-up system. However, adding these positions will require effective training programs to ensure volunteers are well prepared for such tasks.

A further immediate need is effective resourcing for the project, particularly in the area of transport and cash for minor needs such as reimbursement of volunteers out of pocket expenses. Training such as that identified is readily available at reasonable rates and finance would be needed in this area, too.

There is also a need to establish, with firstly the ownership and management and then the staff of this facility, a new foundation on which their project is based and the degree to which the facility is able to provide additional support and clarity of purpose. Engaging the management and staff in such a process may raise points of tension that would need expert negotiation. It is likely that the essence of the developmental nature of the project could be lost if it is subsumed too much into the culture and machinery of the facility and its ultimate goals and its business, political and industrial environment.

Reaching out

At the next level, Mike and Washuntara's vision is that the Circle of Men model might be transposed to other aged care facilities within the Redland City. This part of the vision is based on demands already being expressed by other facilities. Clarifying the exact nature of the outcomes expected and the methods involved for transposing Circle of Men groups in other aged care facilities would seem a complex task. A subsequent issue to be explored would be the degree to which it is advisable, or even likely, that others could replicate the Circle of Men model. It is quite possible that other facilities may well want to influence the model in other directions. The logistics that are likely to be involved in setting up, supporting and maintaining teams of facilitators and assistants for Circle of Men groups would also be a complex task.

Establishing the infrastructure

The advantages in forming a network of Circle of Men projects in most or all aged care facilities in the one area would seem to be the ongoing sustainability of the Circle of Men model, as well as providing different layers of integrated support and resources for teams in individual facilities. Such a web would need to be underpinned by the incorporation of an independent organisation with a suitable organisational structure.

Community development emphasizes the importance of stabilising developmental work within the context of an appropriate organisation that clearly has the capacity and flexibility for supporting the special nature of such delicate work. This involves ensuring that the organisation:
- has a formal commitment to and experience in working developmentally
- has the organisational and legal structure for working developmentally
- can manage and maintain the internal and external factors that may impact upon working developmentally.

Such an organisation would need to operate as a central hub for the training and supply of the Circle of Men teams for each facility. It would also double as a focus point for community activities and events, thus breaking down the practice of all activities for residents being concentrated within the aged care facilities alone. This base could provide a point for residents to meet and interact with a cross section of the wider community and act as a medium for facilitating resident engagement in a range of groups and activities in the 'real' world. Such a base would need its own adequate and ongoing capacity for sustainability, primarily to ensure its independence.

An aged care providers group, consisting of the owners and managers of the aged care facilities in the Redland City, presently exists. It acts as a forum for owners and managers to work and lobby around common concerns, notwithstanding the competitive basis to their existence. The question arises as to whether this group could initiate the system of Circle of Men groups that would include the attendant home base concept. It is Mike and Washuntara's belief that the possibility for conflicts of interest would be too great if undertaken by this providers group, and that the need to preserve a developmental or bottom-up approach to the program overall would be compromised.

It is therefore proposed that an independent hub organisation would best be able to meet the special criteria discussed and might also function as a much needed independent monitor (watchdog) of the overall social well-being of residents in aged care facilities. This model could address much of the other forms of social isolation that presently exists and is largely tolerated in many facilities.

Whatever the future, Mike and Washuntara have thrown the spotlight on an issue that, with the onward march of a burgeoning ageing population in Australia, has grave proportions. They have demonstrated some of the necessities of ensuring that the social and emotional needs of older people are met. For this, they and their team of volunteers deserve considerable commendation and recognition for the time, energy and love that they have contributed to establishing and growing the Circle of Men.

References

De Beauvoir, S. (1972). *Old age*. London: Deutsch, Weidenfeld and Nicolson.

Dept of Health and Ageing. (2003). *Commonwealth aged care guide: Monitoring aged care standards*. Retrieved from http://healthconnect.gov.au

Dept of Health and Ageing. (2004). *Standards for aged care facilities*. Retrieved from http://www.health.gov.au

Frank, F. & Smith, A. (1999). *The community development handbook: A tool to build community capacity*. Quebec: Ministry for Public Works and Government Services.

Friere, P. (1973). *Education for critical consciousness*. London: Sheed and Ward.

Goffmann, E. (1969). *The presentation of self in everyday life*. London: Allen Lane.

Goffmann, E. (1968). *Asylums: Essays on the social situation of mental patients and other inmates*. Harmondsworth: Penguin Books.

Ife, J. (2002). *Community development: Community based alternatives in an age of globalisation*. Frenchs Forest: Pearson Education

Kelly, A. & Sewell, S. (1988). *With head heart and hand: Dimensions of community building*. Brisbane: Boolarong Press.

O'Rielly, M., Courtney, M., & Edwards, H. (2007). How is quality being monitored in Australian residential aged care facilities? A narrative review. *International Journal for Quality in Health Care, 19*(3), 177-182.

Queensland Nurses Union. (2004). *Why aged care needs nurses.* Retrieved from http://www.qnu.org.au

Redlands Shire Council. (2006). *Ageing well in the Redlands: A ten year strategy for seniors.* Retrieved from http://www.redlands.qld.gov.au

Venturato, L., Kellett, U., & Windsor, C. (2007). Nurses' experiences of practice and political reform in long-term aged care in Australia: Implications for the retention of nursing personnel: Working in a changing care environment. *Journal of Nursing Management, 15*(1), 4-11.

Chapter 4
The Circle of Men

A Commentary

Karen Finlay, Mark Creyton and Ann Ingamells

This chapter has contributions from three people. Karen Finlay witnessed the development and struggles of the Circle of Men from her position within the Community Development section of Redland Shire Council. Mark Creyton, from Volunteering Queensland was supportive of the Circle of Men and appreciated it as a capacity building process. Ann Ingamells, an editor, weaves the chapter together with some comments on method.

Labonte (1998) argues that community development is something workers do, whereas when the people of the community act, it is not usually, or necessarily, with technical knowledge of community development as a method of social practice. Mike and Washuntara, as community residents, began this project from their desire to do something to ease what they saw and felt as an intolerable situation. Although both through their lives had gained significant knowledge of the social practices of the public world, their response to this issue in their community was grassroots, intuitive, and unfettered by the kinds of constraints a professional would face. For example, keen to act, they resisted drawn out planning sessions and committee deliberations, and simply turned up at a residential facility and offered their services. Later, impatient with private providers of nursing care, Washuntara spoke his mind to them, in ways that posed a risk to the broader work of patiently developing local relationships and advocacy strategies. Speaking truth to power is something community members can do when they figure there is little to lose, but it is rarely a possibility for professionals who have organisational reputations and longer term strategies to protect.

The power of this community project is that it is not run by professionals. It is run by men who are aware of their own social conditioning as men and are empathic towards the situation of older men in residential care. In terms of the implicate method in the framework provided by Athena Lathouras in Chapter 2, it is instructive that to date Mike's and Washuntara's internal worldviews have been consistent with their actions. They joined from the point of their vulnerability as men with the men in the facility. To move from social and emotional distance to relationship, fun, enjoyment, together was the initial aim. This implicate connection was both strength and limiting factor. To shift the project to formal volunteer and organisational space threatens this delicate implicate order, and whilst rationally they want to grow the project, at another level, they are hanging on, not wanting to lose what is at its heart.

Structuring the circle of men as a volunteer program within an existing organisation will have a number of advantages and disadvantages. Karen Finlay was watching this process of the Circle of Men from her position in the Community Development section of Redland Shire Council. From that vantage point it seems that the sustainability of the activity is best met through a structured volunteer program.

A commentary on Circle of Men

Karen Finlay

I have never been to a Circle of Men gathering, nor would I want to intrude on what is essentially 'private men's business'. My focus in the Circle of Men project isn't about how Mike and Washuntara got to where they are now, but the transformation phase about to begin that will take the Circle of Men project from grass roots innovation and delivery, to sustainable community service.

Mike and Washuntara have indeed reached that 'fork in the road', recognising the positive outcomes achieved for the men in one aged care facility, can (and should) be shared to help others. They have also recognised they need help to fulfil that vision. Anyone who has ever flown on a commercial airline can probably recall what they need to do if the air mask drops from the ceiling. The key instruction is ... *fit your own mask first, then assist others*. The process Mike and Washuntara are about to undertake is about fitting their own masks securely so they may grow stronger and indeed be able to assist many more men.

Circle of Men – then, now and soon

Men's support groups have existed informally for a long time. Except they weren't called 'support groups', it was just a group of blokes spinning a yarn around the campfire. Men's groups became popular in the early 1990s when American author and early pioneer of the Men's Movement, Bill Kauth, wrote the original 'bible' for creating men's groups, *A Circle of Men* (1992). It is from these beginnings that I assume Washuntara has taken inspiration.

My great envy about grass roots projects, like the Circle of Men, is their ability to be exclusively innovative and responsive in their approach to satisfying individual needs. Mike and Washuntara have so far been able to work independently, unfettered by doctrine imposed by an overarching organisation – regardless of whether that organisation is community-based, private or public sector. The next phase of growth for the Circle of Men project will introduce Mike and Washuntara to new operational concepts around organised volunteering and governance, and given the challenges ahead, they are taking the right approach by seeking out help and support.

In Australia, more than 60% of volunteering is 'unorganised' – that is, informal, unpaid help usually provided by family, friends and neighbours (Ironmonger, 2006, p. 10). To handle the growth in volunteer numbers, Mike and Washuntara will change their service delivery status from unorganised to 'organised' volunteering. Organised volunteering is unpaid help in the form of time, service or skills willingly given by an individual through an organisation or group (Ironmonger, 2006, p. 2).

So how will this change affect Mike and Washuntara and the Circle of Men project?

In 2001, Volunteering Australia released *A National Agenda on Volunteering*, which recognised

• Many volunteers are exposed to risk, injury, discrimination or prejudice ... others carry huge financial responsibility or are exposed to legal liability. It is in the interests of all Australians that volunteers are protected under law (p. 5).

The advantage of participating in organised volunteering is the protection it offers to both volunteers and clients through good *governance* practices. Critics complain governance is limiting, restrictive and an unnecessary imposition. However, it is the foundation from which community groups and organisations can build sustainability and success. Governance involves setting a clear vision and direction for the Circle of Men as well as establishing the managerial structures and systems needed to guide the project to achieve its immediate and long-term goals. The Circle of Men group will now need to concern themselves with legal compliance, risk management, accountability, obligations to volunteers and, if on the road to becoming an incorporated organisation, recruiting appropriately skilled committee members.

There is no doubt the world today is a different place for volunteers. No longer is volunteering just about fulfilling an altruistic desire to do a good deed for another. Volunteers today undergo background security checks (police checks, positive notice for working with children/disabled) before they can be accepted as a volunteer. Whilst unpaid, volunteers must adhere to a Position Description, Code of Conduct and apply work-place occupational health and safety standards. They must understand and exercise their obligations under Duty of Care. For legal purposes, volunteers are 'workers' (Herd, 2005) and weighed down with this much responsibility, they probably feel like a worker. So should we be surprised when organisations report they can't attract volunteers? Barriers to recruiting volunteers have been reported as:

• attracting and recruiting suitable volunteers
• skills and training
• lack of organisational capacity to recruit, engage and manage volunteers
• the costs and administration associated with complying with legislative and procedural requirements
• costs to volunteers

(Volunteering Australia, 2007, p. 2)

Older volunteers tell me about another barrier ... 'volunteering isn't *fun* any more'. With so many barriers to contend with, Mike and Washuntara have an even more difficult challenge to recruit predominantly male volunteers. Taken from the ABS Voluntary Work Australia 2000 Statistics – Queensland:

• There are fewer male volunteers - 45.6% (this declines to 38.8% for older male volunteers aged 65 and over)
• a relatively low 22.4% of all volunteers participate in an activity that includes befriending, supporting, listening or counselling

(Volunteering Queensland, 2007)

Respecting the delicate and intimate nature of the work undertaken by the Circle of Men volunteers, one significant challenge will be managing their duty of care responsibilities. According to lawyer Brian Herd (2005, p. 6)

• Duty of care = law of legal relationships or reliance (e.g. organisation to volunteer; volunteer to client).

In law, a 'duty' is when someone's action, or inaction, could reasonably be expected to affect someone else. Failing to meet the standards that a reasonable person would meet in the same circumstances constitutes a breach of this duty. Volunteering mythology decrees volunteers carry no legal status and are therefore untouchable. This is incorrect. Volunteers carry significant legal responsibilities. The connection between organised volunteering and good governance is now very clear.

The awareness of the need for good governance and solid volunteer management is growing in the community sector. Instead of taking a huge personal risk by doing it all themselves, Mike and Washuntara are to be congratulated for seeking out the help they need to expand this project in a safe and sustainable way. All effective volunteer programs operate with some risk; it is now Mike and Washuntara's challenge to manage that risk as the group grows. For small groups like the Circle of Men, *partnering* with an experienced community organisation like RDCOTA is critically important during a transformation phase.

Mike and Washuntara are committed to, and passionate about, the work delivered through the Circle of Men. The road ahead is daunting, but Mike and Washuntara will refuse to say 'it can't be done'. They have fitted their masks securely and won't shy away from finding a way to better serve men and protect their volunteers. That's what effective volunteer groups do.

The Circle of Men Project as community capacity building

By Mark Creyton, Manager Education and Research, Volunteering Queensland

Writing on community development and community capacity building has been proliferating, informed by many streams of writing in the fields of community work, environment, community development, health and community planning.

Chaskin (2003, p. 6) provides one of the clearer definitions of community capacity as: 'the interaction of human capital, organizational resources and social capital existing within a given community that can be leveraged to solve collective problems and improve or maintain the wellbeing of a given community. It may operate through informal social processes and/or organized effort'.

While the literature is incredibly varied, there appear to be some common key elements to a community / capacity building approach especially within grassroots and local based initiatives (Creyton, See and Bourke, 2005). Let us consider the Circle of Men Project with regard to six elements of effective capacity building: asset focus, relationship driven, local nature of initiatives, community engagement and empowerment, inclusion and sustainability.

1. Asset focus

Capacity Building identifies and builds on the assets and strengths within the community. Each segment of the community from families, businesses, governments, schools, faith based institutions, associations, organisations have various commitments, skills and resources to contribute to capacity building and, in partnership, each gains in capacity (Mayer, 2002).

The project works with a group of men whose strengths, interests and capacities have been ignored to a point where they have lost confidence and feel isolated. Through discussions, outings and activities the men begin to re-discover their own sense of an active engaged self, as someone who can contribute within the group and the broader community.

2. Relationships driven

Capacity Building is relationship driven. It utilises, builds and extends on networks, partnerships and alliances. This includes valuing and supporting informal networks and the variety of relationships already existing within communities as well as acknowledging the importance of relational leadership.

One of the key success factors in this project has been focus on facilitating and supporting the building of relationships between the men, on a collective inclusive approach rather than a client centred individual approach. This has been a long process, which included re-building the men's own capacity for listening and communicating. At the same time other individuals and groups are being involved in the program to extend the interactions, relationships and spheres of interests that the men are engaged in.

3. Local nature of initiatives

A focus on assets and strengths within communities, which are driven and fostered by relationships and networks, requires a strong internal focus 'stressing the primacy of local definition, investment, creativity hope and control' (Kretzmann and McKnight, 1993). Capacity building emphasises local, bottom-up initiatives that are embedded in the community. 'Capacity building should supplement and support existing initiatives rather than take over from other community development processes' (Sustainable Communities Network, 2003, p. 19)

Local issues require local knowledge, leaders and management. To be sustainable it must be community driven.

The men reside in the same aged care facility and the program has made a focus of a very local, grounded approach, which reflects the lived experience of the men and works flexibly with the individuals involved. The program has made an extensive effort to involve the local community and to engage the men back in the local community.

4. Community empowerment and engagement

Capacity building goes beyond community consultation and involvement. Community empowerment may include development of shared vision and recognition of shared history, large-scale community involvement, community ownership, direction setting and decision making. A key outcome of these processes is a greater sense of connectedness across the community.

At the heart of this program is empowerment and engagement. Through involving the men in all aspects of the program including the planning, through meeting individual needs through a collective process, through ensuring the program remains flexible and developmental and responsive to the men's different needs and interests.

5. Inclusion

Inclusion is a key principle in much of the capacity building thinking. By engaging all groups, including those who have been marginalised, we can:
• identify a range of assets previously not recognised or valued
• gain greater participation which can lead to better solutions and outcomes
• avoid social isolation and disconnection, fostering greater social capital and cohesion

(Bush, Mutch and Dower, 2001; Kretzmann and McKnight, 1993).

Capacity builders need to utilise a variety of processes that identify and engage with groups who are traditionally marginalised, silenced and/or excluded. A key challenge is the process of inclusion which values and ensures diversity and difference (Hashagen, 2002).

Each environment in which we work provides different challenges for inclusion. In this case it is the older men who are isolated in two ways from the broader community through the aged care facility and within the aged care facility being a very small minority group. The project has focused on both building solidarity between the men and introducing a range of initiatives at both bringing the community in and taking the men out into the community.

6. Sustainability

Many of the previous themes link to the idea of sustainable initiatives and communities. The challenges faced by this program regarding resourcing, embedding in the institution, finding on-going volunteers and extending the program, are common, yet the program continues to operate in part because it is local, volunteer driven and manageable.

Capacity building that incorporates these six elements is multifaceted and takes a holistic approach to issues. It utilises strategies which make a long-term difference and works with and develops local knowledge and local resources, seeking to embed effective community problem solving and community action within the local setting.

Mike and Washuntara, the volunteers who facilitate this project, continue to make a remarkable contribution to the lives of these men.

Conclusion

Community activities do not exist in isolation. Rather each effort to bring about change at the community level is part of a broader landscape in which the humaneness and democratic potential of our societies are being shaped. Tentacles from the Circle of Men to the author, Ross Wiseman, in TAFE, to Karen Finlay and others at Redland Shire Council and to Mark Creyton and others at Volunteering Queensland, as well as within the circles of aged care services in Redlands, all sustain and enrich the potential. Small changes lead to bigger questionings and broader action, and cast a critical light on the directions our society is taking. Taken for granted constructions of gender roles are questioned by Mike and Washuntara, as also are the directions being taken by the aged care industry. Plato in fifth century Greece, asked Socrates *Quis custodiet ipsos custodes?* Or 'Who will guard the guards themselves?' That is, who will critically examine those who set our directions? (Wikipedia, 2009). Our every action in community builds our collective awareness of what is really going on, and begs our consideration of whether that is what we want, and if not, what we can do about it.

References

Bush, R., Mutch, A., Dower, J. (2002). *Community Capacity Index Manual.* Brisbane: Centre for Primary Health Care, University of Queensland.

Creyton, M., See, M. and Bourke, P. (2005). *Enhancing the capacity of grassroots groups to engage: Practical initiatives from a community-local government partnership.* International Conference on Community Engagement. Accessed on 30 June 2009 at: http://www.engagingcommunities2005.org/ab-theme-11.html

Hashagen, S. (2002). *Models of community engagement.* Scottish Community Development Association. Accessed on 30 June 2009 at: http://leap.scdc.org.uk/uploads/modelsofcommunityengagement.pdf

Herd, B. (2005). *Handle with care: Volunteers and the law.* Seminar in Bardon on 2 August 2005. Paper by Brian Herd, Carne Reidy Herd Lawyers, Brisbane

Ironmonger, D. (2006). *The economic value of volunteering in Queensland.* Brisbane: State of Queensland (Department of Communities)

Kretzmann, J. and McKnight, J. (1993). *Building communities from the inside out: A path toward finding and mobilizing a community's asset.* Chicago: ACTA Publications.

Labonte, R. (1998). *A community development approach to health promotion.* Paper prepared for Health Board of Scotland.

Mayer, S. (2002). *Building community capacity: How different groups contribute.* Accessed on 30 June 2009 at: www.effectivecommunities.com

Sustainable Communities Network. (2003a). *Community capacity, health inequities and sustainable communities: Draft for discussion.* (Version 1) Accessed on 30 June 2009 at: http://scn.ecu.edu.au/news_publications.php

Volunteering Australia. (2006). *A national agenda on volunteering: Beyond the International Year of Volunteers.* Melbourne: Volunteering Australia Inc.

Volunteering Australia. (2007). *National survey of volunteering issues 2007.* Melbourne: Volunteering Australia Inc.

Volunteering Queensland. (2007). *Volunteer statistics and trends.* Accessed on 19 June 2007 at: http://www.volunteeringqueensland.org.au/information_resources/statistics_trends.shtml

Wikipedia, accessed 08/05/2009 at Wikipedia http://en.wikipedia.org/wiki/Quis_custodiet_ipsos_custodes%3F

Chapter 5

Story of Working with Southern Sudanese refugees within Brisbane and Logan

Peter Westoby

Introduction

For several years and from a variety of roles and organisational bases, I have worked with people who have come to Australia as refugees, and particularly with people from Southern Sudan. During that time, I have endeavoured to work within a community development orientation. I found, however, that the practice of most agencies in the refugee field emphasised individual and family support through case management and therapeutic interventions. Agencies were supported by an authoritative psychiatric literature on post traumatic stress and individual healing from the trauma caused by war, torture and the refugee experience. A catalyst for change occurred when Southern Sudanese people themselves challenged the Western, service delivery practices of the agencies they were engaging with. To meet the challenge, we needed to develop different kinds of relationships, rethink our analyses and approach practice in new ways.

   In this chapter, I recount my efforts to find an analysis and theoretical framework that would better inform community development practice with people who are refugees. A framework was sought that is complex enough to include, but not be dominated by, the psychiatric literature of individual trauma and healing. I also sought a framework that could un-hitch the ties between settlement practices and assumptions based in assimilation. I chose to approach this through PhD research. This was not an individual journey however, for relationships and dialogue with Southern Sudanese people were significant, and the journey also influenced and was influenced by the agency I worked for. Nevertheless, in this account, it is my own story, which I have the authority to tell.

Background

To put the story in context, some of the key stages of my engagement with refugee communities and particularly the South Sudanese community, are outlined here:

Firstly, as a youth worker during the period 1998 to 2000 I was engaged with young people from Sudan under the auspices of a refugee-oriented service delivery organisation. Such work entailed running youth activities, youth camps, developing a home-work support club, engaging in inter-cultural conflict negotiation (between Sudanese young people and other groups of young people), supporting schools in their engagement with Sudanese young people, their families and communities.

Secondly, there was engagement with Sudanese groups as a community development worker from 2001-2004 also under the auspices of the same refugee-oriented service delivery organisation. Such work entailed supporting the development of a Sudanese Elders group, the Sudanese Community Association, a project in inter-generational conflict reduction, the development of a family-in-cultural-transition program and a dialogue-in-healing initiative.

Thirdly, I was engaged with Sudanese leadership as a community trainer during 2004/5 under the auspices of a non-profit cooperative called Community Praxis Co-op. This entailed supporting approximately twenty Sudanese leaders in reflecting on community building and community development processes within their own community and within the broader host community.

Fourthly, there was involvement in project management of an intercultural youth project, 'The Peace Potion' during 2002-2004 as a Community Praxis Co-op consultant. This work entailed brokering and managing an initiative in partnership with the non-profit organisation, Contact Youth Inc. The project involved young people from Sudanese, Polynesian and Indigenous communities in exploring the multiple meanings of peace, conflict and honour in dialogue with one another as a way of building inter-cultural understanding and reducing potential conflict and violence.

Finally there was engagement with the Sudanese community as a researcher from 2003-2006 conducting an action research oriented PhD dissertation that explored 'social processes of healing' as opposed to therapeutically-oriented ones.

While working during 2002/3, I was involved in a project called a 'dialogue-in-healing' that provided the first step onto the ladder of engagement and intellectual work central to the story of this chapter. That initial project involved six different groups of refugees – Somali, El Salvadorian, Iranian, Bosnian, Southern Sudanese and Tibetan. During the course of that project there was an invitation by Southern Sudanese elders to consider a new model of engagement with their community. That journey is the story of this chapter.

Before telling that story though, I will recount something of the events in Sudan and the Sudanese people's experience in coming to Australia. This is important for two reasons. Firstly, I discovered that many workers in the field do not think it important to know the background of the people they work with; yet, I find that having that background information is central to relationship building. Secondly, the analysis of the practitioner is always reflected in the practice. It determines what a practitioner can hear and relate to, and it shapes the kinds of responses which seem relevant. The next section then is just some of the analysis that informs my own practice with South Sudanese people.

The Sudanese story of coming to Australia

Sudan is the largest country in Africa with a population of over 35 million people. This population belongs to between 50 and 100 different ethnic groups and further comprises some 570 distinct peoples. The largest groups – Arab (39%), Dinka (10%), Beja, Nuer, Nuba, Nubian, Fur, Bari, Azande, Moru and Shilluk (in that order) – represent about 75% of the population (Fanjoy M., Ingraham, H., Khoury, C. & Osman, A., 2005, p. 9). Sudan has been in civil war nearly continuously since independence from Britain in 1956 (Rogier, 2005). The civil war has been between the predominantly Islamic, Arabic north and a diversity of African ethnic groups in the south, mainly Christian or Animist (U.S. Committee for Refugees, 2000) caused by what has predominantly been seen as systemic injustices, 'embodied in national policies of forced Arabization and Islamization, compounded by the historic exploitation and neglect of Southern Sudan' (Deng, 2004, p. 9). Sudan is now among the poorest countries in the world, (World Health Organisation, 2000) a result of war induced underdevelopment and impoverishment (Deng, 2004, p. 11). In the late 1980s and early 1990s an escalation in conflict, drought and the imposition of strict Islamic law and Arabic as the official language led to an increase in refugee movement. In 1993 it was estimated that nearly half a million Sudanese found refuge in other countries excluding the 1.3 million estimated to have died in the flight (U.S. Committee for Refugees, 2000).

Refugees from Sudan are composed of numerous ethnic groups from the South as well as political refugees from the North. The Christian community, while being a minority in Sudan, is disproportionately represented in the resettled populations globally. As many as 30,000 children and adolescents were separated from their families during flight to neighbouring countries in the late 1980s. The story *What is the What* (Eggers, 2006) would enlighten any reader as to the experiences of these young people

more thoroughly than any academically-oriented text. Now, in early adult-
hood they also represent a significant proportion of the resettled refugees.

The conflict in Sudan has been analysed traditionally through a North-
South dichotomy rooted in military and political confrontation between
the National Islamic Front (NIF) of Khartoum and the Sudanese People's
LiberationMovement/Army (SPLM/A). Most of the refugees coming to
Australia are Southern Sudanese refugees. Many of them have been active
participants in the conflict as either officers or soldiers in the SPLM/A.
However, more recent history reveals that there are several other fault lines
of conflict – notably conceptualized as East-West (Deng, 2004) or Centre-
Periphery (Rogier, 2005) evidenced in a horrific war in Darfur (Prunier,
2005) and also currently escalating conflict in eastern Sudan (Rogier, 2005).

Southern Sudanese refugees fleeing the country usually travel, through
whatever means available, to either Cairo in Egypt, or Kenya and Uganda,
the places where there are both a significant UNHCR presence and substantial Sudanese communities. For example there are some fifteen thou-
sand Sudanese in Cairo (Fanjoy et al., 2005). Those who travel to Cairo will
then experience urban refugee lives as first asylum seekers. They will enjoy,
to various degrees, the protection of the UNHCR but are forced to live by
whatever means possible constrained or supported by various rights (or
lack of rights) granted by the Egyptian state (Coker, 2004a). Those in
Kenya would have predominantly experienced first asylum within refugee
camps (Kakuma camp being the largest) auspiced by the UNHCR. As first
asylum refugees, and having been granted refugee status by UNHCR, both
groups would then be entitled to apply for resettlement with the programs
of resettling nations such as Australia, USA, Canada and so forth. These
applications would be lodged as part of Australia's Off-Shore Programme
of refugee or humanitarian resettlement.

As of 2007, African communities are the largest intake within Australia's humanitarian and refugee intake from the Off-Shore Programme.
By 2005 there were 23,787 Sudanese living in Australia (Australian Bureau
of Statistics). On arrival in Australia, and for the first six months of settlement, Southern Sudanese refugees have full access to the Integrated Humanitarian Services Strategy (IHSS) provided by a range of social services
funded by the Department of Immigration and Citizenship (DIAC). Some
social and community services also have funding from the Community Services Settlement Scheme (CSSS) enabling them to support refugee groups
in the post-six month period and up to five years after arrival.

Alongside professional services, Southern Sudanese refugees settling
within Brisbane and Logan have also established a diverse infrastructure of
non-formal and formal groups that have many different community functions. The key formal groups within Brisbane and Logan are the Queensland Sudanese Community Association, the Sudanese People's Liberation
Movement/Army (SPLM/A) Brisbane Chapter and the Sudanese Christian
Fellowship. More recently established groups include a Sudanese Women's Association, a youth organisation, several 'ethnic' associations
(representing different tribes), a Lost Boys' Association[1] and several active

cultural groups. While such organisations focus on community life here in Australia many Sudanese also maintain links and an orientation to current struggles within Sudan and other Diaspora groups through informal channels of communication amongst kin, through an electronic Diaspora community network and through official channels such as the SPLM/A representative within Australia. These groups represent much of the official leadership of the community. Such people are doing amazing community work daily – albeit unpaid and voluntary – and of course this work is all mixed up with the pressures of their own settlement processes. There are also many informal leaders and many community members who support new arrivals, who engage in the work of welcome, support, taking people to banks, shops, moving house and so forth.

While there has been no comprehensive academic studies of the Southern Sudanese community within Australia there have been numerous issue focussed studies indicating concerns about the educational gaps of young people in Victoria (Victorian Foundation for Survivors of Torture, VFST, 2005a), the experiences of young Sudanese in Brisbane's public spaces (Youth Affairs Network of Queensland, YANQ, 2005), the experiences of sexual violence amongst Sudanese women (VFST, 2005b), mental health concerns (Schweitzer et al., 2006) and housing concerns (Kelly, 2004). There has also been a plethora of newspaper articles within the Courier Mail, The Sydney Morning Herald, The Age (Melbourne) and The Australian, indicating that the Sudanese are a very visible group now causing multiple concerns and confusions within the broader national body politic.

Returning to the story

During the period 1999-2003, South Sudanese people began questioning the ways organisations were working with them. While many refugees acknowledged the cross-cultural competency of many workers, there was still a sense of a whole other world of non-Western approaches to which no space was given. Communities were not being engaged with on their terms, and ways of knowing and healing, which is part of Sudanese culture, were ignored. Despite their very good intentions, agencies seemed to be stuck in colonial and neo-colonial methodologies of work. Sudanese community leaders invited agencies to engage with them in a spirit of partnership that would enable a more authentic empowering process.

These discussions with South Sudanese people took place in the context of heightened conflict between South Sudanese community members. Conflict within communities, and indeed within families, relate both to

---

1. This association has been formed by young men who have formed part of their identity around the label 'Lost Boys' – a label developed initially by the media. The Lost Boys of Sudan refers to orphaned boys during the war from 1987 on who walked thousands of kilometers from Sudan to Ethiopia, were expelled back to Sudan, and walked to Kenya. Many have been given resettlement places in the USA and Australia.

the conflicts in their country and to the struggles to re-establish in a new
country. War related distress disrupts community and family life, causing
breakdown, intergenerational conflict, and tensions between different
groups in the community. These are exacerbated by religious, tribal, clan,
political, linguistic differences, and a crisis of legitimate leadership. Agencies, careful not to become involved in such conflict, also tended to ignore
it. Growing unease came to a head when several workers were accused in a
public meeting of being part of the 'axis of evil' by several elders of the
Southern Sudanese community. They saw many agency interventions as
contributing to increasing, rather than reducing, pre-existing conflict within their community in Brisbane.

> *You professionals are part of the 'axis of evil' ... you are making our lives more
> difficult....*

> *Your approaches are neo-colonial and causing more conflict in our communities....*

> (Two statements made by Southern Sudanese refugee elders at a public
> meeting)

Members of the Sudanese community claimed we were facilitating the further fragmentation of families through workers supporting women who
wanted to leave their husbands and enabling young people who wanted to
leave home to find alternative sources of accommodation. Organisations
were accused of operating independently of both formal and informal
Sudanese leadership in ways that undermined that leadership and therefore
damaged community cohesion.

As practitioners we were upset in clearly not meeting the first principle
of practice, which is to do no harm. Several people in the organisation were
interested in exploring ways to realign its practice, and I particularly
wanted to strengthen my own ability to respond to the Sudanese community. The agency, however, worked with many communities, and many
people experienced its approach as helpful. A community development approach suggested that the first step would be for the agency to acknowledge the concerns of the Sudanese people and their invitation, and endeavour to form an agreement with the Sudanese people that they would work
with them to bring about change. This was achieved and led to a few
changes such as a Sudanese person being appointed onto the Board of
Management, and employment of a Sudanese worker, but beyond that we
were unclear where to go.

It was not only the agency and I who were uncertain of direction. The
South Sudanese had a clear critique of our practice, but did not have a clear
idea of where they or we should be going. This was not articulated at the
time, but some time later an elder commented:

> *Our current culture is acting as a guide in ways that seem to create mistrust, constant
> criticism and power struggles. We feel lost and need some help in reorienting our
> culture.*

Dialogue was the one tool we had available to us as a way forward. Several
Southern Sudanese elders who had participated in the original Dialogue-
In-Healing project were very supportive of more extensive dialogue.

Dialogue is more than just talking, it is rather a purposeful approach to addressing difficult issues between people who are not necessarily in agreement, but who have a shared interest in finding a way forward.

As a part of this dialogue several Sudanese leaders set up a meeting with an informal group that included other elders, the leaders of the Queensland Sudanese Community Association (including the Logan City Branch), the Sudanese Christian Fellowship and the Brisbane Chapter of the Sudanese People's Liberation Movement/ Army (SPLM/A). For them, this was a significant moment in their relationship with services, of moving from being recipients of individualised services to inviting us to engage with them in the issues confronting them. For me, this moment was the crux of re-structuring towards community development methods. Up until now, we the professionals had been driving a process of engagement – albeit as sensitively as we could, but now the focus of control had shifted. We had been identifying the needs – now the Sudanese leadership was entering into a dialogue about those needs.

With the support of my agency and the Sudanese community I decided to go part time at work and undertake a PhD, which would both track the dialogue as it emerged and also establish what, in the literature, could help us establish a more appropriate framework for agencies to work with the Sudanese or other refugee communities.

Some of the complexities of working with refugee groups are apparent when I reflect on what happened here. Firstly, this was a shift in power relations. To this point, the agency and workers had maintained an agenda that held them clear of the complexities. This challenge and shift made it more difficult to maintain distance from the complexities of settlement, conflict and community relations. We, the professionals no longer knew what to do, any better than the community members themselves did. Secondly, some key leaders, elders as mainly males, had structured their relationships to the point where they felt bold enough to challenge the very welfare-oriented services that they were somewhat dependent on. As workers committed to developmental processes it was important to honour that developmental process and start a new dialogue based on a new kind of relationship. There was a significant shift from what we would call a service relationship to a 'developmental relationship' in that there was a mutual agreement to try and do something 'together'.

As practitioners we were excited by the opportunity to engage with members of the South Sudanese in this way. However, an uncomfortable aspect for me was that we already had relationships with, and commitments to, young people and women in that community. We knew that the elders and male leaders reflected one perspective – and that some young people and women would have quite different perspectives. For several of us it remained important to continue to build developmental relationships with other members of the community. We wanted to support young people and women in their settlement and leadership development processes, while still respecting the customary leadership of the community. This placed us within a complex web of relationships, where we could

63

easily lose the trust of one or other groups. Yet it also enabled us to see and acknowledge how the differing needs of different groups cause conflict, and assist people to hear and understand each other. Our position was tolerable to the elders because they had already been exposed to dialogue as a tool to assist them to hear their young people and be heard by them.

As part of my work within the youth team of the agency I had already established a brokering role between the needs and aspirations of the Sudanese and the agendas or lack of agendas of the education system. The youth work team had worked closely with young people, their parents and elders in doing this, trying to create a bridge between the community, (which had many fears about the education system) and schools (which, with community input, could provide the conditions for young people to bridge the two communities in which they will make their way in life).

For several previous years we had been working with young people on their agendas. Now I had been invited to work with leaders on their agendas, and it was clear there were different agendas at stake and conflict between them. Once again, dialogue is one way of building bridges across competing and conflicting agendas. It is likely to work best where the relationships are important and certainly the relationships to their young people were important to the Sudanese elders.

The following section describes some of the literature and concepts, which informed both my PhD work and my effort to find a better framework for practice.

Towards a new analysis

The PhD allowed something of a reflexive pause, with time to read, access new literature, and think through some of the deeper issues of engagement between a western culture and a refugee community. My aim was to provide a direction for the work that my agency and myself were engaged in which would be compatible with what the community was asking for.

I began my reading by seeking material that provided critique of the dominant practice frameworks. I had observed that practice was driven, often not intentionally or explicitly, by a therapeutic orientation. To my surprise, the very strong emphasis on psychiatric models of trauma accompanied by practices focussed on individual healing was soundly critiqued by members of the psychiatric professions themselves. Patrick Bracken (2002) argued that therapeutic culture medicalises distress leading to a reliance on professional and clinical intervention. Such psychiatrists as Bracken (2002) and Derek Summerfield (1999) recognise that the labelling of refugees as traumatised means that the *injury* is the focus of intervention and the wider social world of the person or group receives less attention. Summerfield specifically argues that refugees have suffered dislocation from their social world, and rebuilding this is as important as, and even crucial to, psychological healing. Yet, so powerful is the medical model, that all resources follow its diagnoses.

The more individuals and groups are labelled vulnerable, 'at risk' or as having 'special needs', the less empowered the person feels to act on their own situation, and the more empowered the professional is to intervene. Frank Furedi (2005) argues that there is a conservative trend towards 'therapeutic culture' in which increasing numbers of groups are labelled 'at risk', caught within discourses of vulnerability and powerlessness, and as a result of this, such groups suffer diminished agency. There is a conflict then between such discourses and the needs of refugee groups to establish agency in their new context.

Significantly, this language of therapeutics has often been employed by refugee groups themselves and their advocates, in supporting their claims to resources and entitlements. Policymakers are more likely to respond to groups who suffer trauma and are at risk, than to groups who are engaged in regaining agency and rebuilding community. Yet casting oneself as injured and as victim can be very disempowering and can work against the goals such communities seek.

These critics of the dominant therapeutic discourse, all imply that refugee recovery is a social process as much as an individual and psychological process. The critical task is to rebuild the social world. This includes establishing a place to live, coming to see it as home, addressing issues of schooling, livelihood, and family functioning. It also includes finding social meaning in the new context, grappling with issues of social values, and engaging social relationships.

The refugee experiences of forced migration and resettlement involve an even more significant disruption to a social world – one could even say complete rupture. Social relationships are fragmented and lost; kin, extended family and other social networks crumble under the weight of dislocation. Refugee war related suffering is reinforced by migration related loss (Hoffman, 2004; Brough et al., 2003). Other authors have described this as shock, fracture and bereavement (Schweitzer, Buckley and Rossi, 2002; Silove, 1999).

The combinations of these analyses, and my dialogues with South Sudanese people suggested that only a very small part of the refugee struggle is supported by funding and agency practices. Refugee communities struggle on a number of fronts with things which most of us take for granted. As well as dealing with dislocation, grief, mourning and loss, other fronts of refugee struggle include:

- rebuilding the social world
- acquiring sufficient social and political agency to influence the various situations one finds oneself within
- the need for community – a sense of belonging, both with people of one's own culture and people in the host community, enjoyable and supportive relationships with people outside the family
- protecting one's children and young people, marriage, family, from the strange values of the host culture

- engaging in the social and political processes of two cultures in an ongoing way
- engaging or not with their own community here in relation to ongoing wars at home
- and for some, especially children and women, gaining enough freedom from family and culture to survive the new environments (like school, work) of the new social setting, whilst maintaining the love and support of family.

Agencies do often assist with social supports around housing, employment and education. They do engage with refugee communities in celebrating culture, and they do support the development of community. Yet, for various reasons of political and professional legitimacy, these activities tend to remain marginal to the dominant discourse of trauma and individualised healing. A framework, which emphasised rebuilding the social world would emphasise empowerment and agency. A framework, which emphasised community, would emphasise both bonding and bridging relations within and across various communities. A framework, which emphasised culture, would emphasise social meaning, and issues of identity and belonging.

A community development practice approach would draw direction from these three frameworks, much more readily than from a therapeutically-oriented one.

Giving the analysis legs

Clearly this analysis signposts a few critical issues for re-thinking community development practice. The question is how to action it?

The first signpost emerging from such an analysis is that understanding an individual's distress needs to be located within a broader framework of the social. For example, while a refugee might express their distress as depression, the issues may be to do with the loss of their social world.

The analysis invites community practitioners to avoid utilising a discourse of victim and vulnerability and be very careful when we use the language of trauma. We need to be more conscious that when using labels such as at-risk or special needs within their broader therapeutic context we are potentially masking the structural processes of marginalisation that cause distress. Conversely we need to focus on the structural and social dimensions of distress and in turn focus on Sudanese agency in bringing about social change. The analysis clarifies that the role of the community development worker is to nurture and support such agency.

While such signposts indicate a way forward in terms of my social analysis they also provide important pointers for supporting refugee agencies in developing their own 'community analysis' (Westoby & Dowling, 2009). Analysis requires engagement with language and key words – it requires the unpacking of meaning, potential masking, and many social dynamics. Supporting refugees in their dialogue around the meanings of such words as trauma and depression, at-risk or special need, requires a re-consideration of them as verbs within a social context rather than simply allowing them to stand as nouns that define reality. Questions can be asked such as, 'What is depression-causing?' 'Why are groups labelled at-risk?' 'Who is doing the labelling?' and 'What is the agenda?' The posing of such questions is central to the process of supporting community analysis.

The on-going story

1. Using a dialogical methodology of intervention

As a community development practitioner, while conscious of the above analysis (emerging from the literature) the challenge was to bring the analysis to the dialogue process with the diverse members of the Sudanese community. They had challenged practices which were not working for them, they would only be open to the kinds of analysis I was developing if it helped them articulate the things they were experiencing. My analysis was to some extent a social analysis. That is, I was trying to understand the things they were telling me, by putting them into the context of broader social forces discussed in the literature. In community development terms the Sudanese people would be enabled to act in their own interests to the extent that they had a shared community analysis. That is an analysis of how these forces operate locally within their community and between their community and the host community. This is what Paulo Freire (1970) called 'conscientisation'. As indicated earlier in the paper, Sudanese elders and leadership had an analysis that was a critique, albeit legitimate critique of our neo-colonial practice, but they often felt stuck in trying to develop a way forward.

Engaged around the questions of how a worker or agency can support them to rebuild their social world, their community or their cultural life, they immediately become more enabled. We engaged together in a series of six workshops co-facilitated by a bi-cultural Sudanese worker and myself. These workshops were open, dynamic conversations that enabled people as a group to make sense of their concerns within a contextual framework. That is – issues were identified, the force fields affecting those issues were discussed, possible solutions were tabled, and actions were tasked.

These facilitated conversations, in the form of workshops, enabled the leadership to move from a robust stance of 'us/them', 'colonial/anti-colonial' to a more tentative dialogical phase of 'with/amongst/within'. Within these workshops there was a desire to talk about, make sense of, and develop a community analysis that was more hopeful. In my experience as a worker, if we do not move developmentally into such a phase of dialogue then the alternative (that usually results from a lack of dialogical engagement) is to remain stuck in 'either/or' scenarios of either ossifying 'Sudanese' cultural, social and political resources, or conversely, completely assimilating into supposed Australian ones, simply reinforcing cycles and sequences of cultural disorientation and social distress. Dialogue creates a space, a new platform for avoiding these 'either/or scenarios', a platform that takes seriously the need to rebuild a new social world.

2. Taking an elicitive stance

Informed by my ongoing engagement with the literature, I was more confident in taking an elicitive stance to facilitation. This stance is theoretically underpinned by the work of John Paul Lederach (1995) who works in the field of cross-cultural conflict transformation. The assumption behind the approach is that there is what I have called an 'agonistic'[2] conflict between the social world 'left' behind as a result of forced migration and the 'new' social world of resettlement. An elicitive stance of facilitation sees the primary mode of community development work as a mutual 'journey of discovery' with all participants including the community development worker learning along the way. The key point is that as a worker we engage in genuine dialogue whereby the worker is as 'in-the-dark' as other participants about possible solutions. The facilitated conversations are literally a process of trying to co-create and co-discover solutions together.

Again, this entailed a deconstructive movement away from the binary of either 'assimilation' or 'rejection'. Hence the emerging process of the deconstructive movement is discovery – in which the cultural, communal and political resources available to Southern Sudanese refugees, albeit disrupted ones, are re-constituted, re-invented, re-oriented, recycled, re-patterned and re-structured in the new context. The role of the worker within the workshops and any on-going post-workshop support is as catalyst for the thoughtful rebuilding of these re-invented (oriented, cycled, patterned, structured) models that constitute the re-building of a new social world.

Within this process of community development the facilitated conversations and on-going post-workshop support resulted in discreet projects that explored: new and recycled ways of parenting; ways of reducing intergenerational conflict, strategies to reduce inter-cultural youth-related conflict, approaches to tackle systemic problems in relation to educational systems, and the development of new structures and practices of Sudanese community organisation.

3. Nurturing structural links

---

2. Agonistic conflict is characterised by a capacity of conflicting parties to remain respectful of one another. It is contrasted with antagonistic conflict where parties move to positions of disrespect (Mouffe, 2005).

As a community development worker it was important to not only have enough structural space to work directly with the Sudanese community on their terms, but to also maintain structural links with various community organisations (service providers and more developmentally-oriented organisations). The rationale for this is that as community workers we need to ensure that the voices and analysis of community members can be translated into organisational responses, not just an individual community development worker response. Community development requires workers to not only support activities that build community and community action, but also to support actions that ensure the re-structuring of organisations towards community. My work with this community required that I continue to liaise structurally with a few organisations through: firstly having regular mandated meetings (that is, we did not just set them up informally, but formally in consultation with the directors of those organisations) with managers of various programs or organisational units that were working with the Sudanese community, enabling me to share action research findings; secondly to circulate several documents (written up from the workshops discussed above) to organisations that contained the community's analysis; and finally through conducting on-going group supervision with workers from numerous organisations enabling people to reflect structurally on their work orientation.

The outcomes and conclusion

So where has all this led? What are some of the outcomes of this story? Well, firstly it is important to state that it is an on-going story. Anyone following the newspapers in recent months would be aware that now the Sudanese population has reached a significant number, they are attracting attention. Most of that attention is focused on 'problems' – often youth related, but also to do with gender, inter-cultural tension, and so forth.

Secondly, it would be arrogant and deceptive to argue that one story has contributed to significant change. There have been so many people, professional and non-professional (citizens, volunteers, church members), who have engaged with Sudanese groups. In many ways it is the combined energies and synergies of these relationships and processes that have brought useful change.

However, there are some key outcomes from this work that are worth stating:

For Southern Sudanese

There are a growing number of leaders that understand the process of engaging their own community in the process of reorienting and rebuilding cultural, communal and political resources. There is an assertive openness to dialogue with workers that now are trusted to be committed to the development journey in an ongoing way.

For organisations

It is difficult for an organisation to change its approach to practice based on a challenge from one community. There is always much invested in an approach to practice, including particular professional orientations, knowledge and frameworks of existing staff. In this case, what proved helpful was to acknowledge, to make some changes, and to create safe spaces for ongoing dialogue. Organisations build relational credibility through on-going engagement, listening, learning and through willingness to resource processes, which are of importance to the community. Employing and appointing Sudanese to key professional (staff) and voluntary positions (management committee) was important to structural credibility.

The challenge remains for organisations of ensuring some ongoing structural engagement with refugee groups. One of the key challenges to engagement is the constant change. New arrivals settle in Australia weekly, new leaders emerge from such cohorts of settlers; older leaders get weary of the demands made upon them by other community members. On top of that, staff regularly changes. So, relationships need to be re-built in all directions. Organisations cannot afford to have engaged for a year, made relationships and then settle back into routine. The constant cycles of settlement and organisational change require systematic ways of re-engaging constantly, re-building relationships, re-challenging assumptions and being willing to move developmentally with initiatives arising from their communities.

For myself as practitioner

I have much greater clarity around how to engage the territory of refugee-related work in terms of the purposes of community development work - rebuilding a social world; the outcomes - reconstituting cultural, communal and political resources; and the methods guided by developmental, dialogical and deconstructive approaches.

My relationships with members of the South Sudanese community are strengthened, including, elders, leaders, women and young people. These relationships are now strengthened through informal, social, and personal communication as well as through formal work. Formal work is now usually by invitation from the Sudanese community to work with them on some initiative of theirs.

Yes there is so much to do, both formally and informally. The journey continues.

References

Bracken, P. (2002). *Trauma, culture, meaning & philosophy*. England: Whurr Publishers.

Brough, M., Gorman, D., Ramirez, E., Westoby, P. (2003). Young refugees talk about well-being. *Australian Journal of Social Issues, 38*(2), 193-208.

Coker, E. M. (2004a). Travelling pains: Embodied metaphors of suffering among Southern Sudanese refugees in Cairo. *Journal of Culture, Medicine and Psychiatry, 28*, 15-39.

Deng, D. (2004). Self reckoning: Challenges of socio-cultural reconstruction and unity in Southern Sudan. *UNICEF.*

Eggers, D. (2006). *What is the what: Autobiography of Valentino Achak Deng.* San Francisco: McSweeney's.

Fanjoy, M., Ingraham, H., Khoury, C. & Osman, A. (2005). Expectations and experiences of resettlement: Sudanese refugees' perspectives of their journeys from Egypt to Australia, Canada and the United States. *Forced Migration and Refugee Studies Program.* Egypt: The American University of Cairo, August 2005. Retrieved at http://www.aucegypt.edu/academic/fmrs/Reports.htm#research on 1.2.06.

Freire, P. (1970). *Pedagogy of the oppressed.* New York: SeaburyPress.

Furedi, F. (2004). *Therapy culture: Cultivating vulnerability in an uncertain age.* London and New York: Routledge.

Hoffman, E. (2004). *After such knowledge: Memory, history & the legacy of the Holocaust.* New York: Public Affairs.

Kelly, E. (2004). *A new country but no place to call home: The experiences of refugee and asylum seekers in housing crisis and strategies for improved housing outcomes.* Victoria: Hanover Welfare Services.

Lederach, J. P. (1995). *Preparing for peace: Conflict transformation across cultures.* New York: Syracuse University Press.

Mouffe, C. (2005). *On the political: Thinking in action.* London & New York: Routledge Press.

Prunier, G. (2005). *Darfur: The ambiguous genocide.* London: Hurst & Company.

Rogier, E. (2005). *No more hills ahead? The Sudan's tortuous ascent to heights of peace.* Clingendael: Netherlands Institute of International Relations. Retrieved at http://www.clingendael.nl/publications/2005/20050800_cscp_security_paper_1.pdf on 1.11.05.

Schweitzer, R., Buckley, L. & Rossi, D. (2002). The psychological treatment of refugees and asylum seekers: What does the literature tell us? *MOTS PLURIELS, 21.* Retrieved at www.arts.uwa.edu.au/MotsPluriels on 5.3.05.

Summerfield, D. (1999). A critique of seven assumptions behind psychological trauma programmes in war-affected areas. *Social Science and Medicine, 48,* 1449-1462.

U.S. Committee for Refugees. (2000). *World refugee survey 2000.* Washington, DC.

Victorian Foundation for Survivors of Torture (VFST). (2005a). Education and refugee students from Southern Sudan. *Victorian Foundation for Survivors of Torture.* Retrieved at www.survivorsvic.org.au on 13.1.06.

VFST. (2005b). Sexual violence and refugee women from west and central Africa. *Victorian Foundation for Survivors of Torture.* Retrieved at www.survivorsvic.org.au on 13.1.06.

Westoby, P. & Dowling, G. (2009). *Dialogical community development: With depth, solidarity and hospitality.* London & West End: Tafina Press.

World Health Organisation. *Healthy life expectancy rankings.* Retrieved at http://www-nt.who.int/whosis/statistics on October, 14, 2000.

Youth Affairs Network of Queensland (YANQ). (2005). *Young Sudanese and public space in Brisbane.* Retrieved at http://www.yanq.org.au/index.pl?page=online_pub on 10.10.05.

Chapter 6
A Sense of a Whole Other World

Worldviewing and Ethical Collaboration across Social Worlds

Polly Walker, John Diew, Di Zetlin

> *Culture is like an underground river; it is full of life, dynamic, and powerful in shaping the course of conflicts, yet often outside our awareness (LeBaron, 2003, p. 3).*

> *...as long as human beings and the societies they form continue to recognize only surface culture and avoid the underlying primary culture, nothing but unpredictable explosions and violence can result (Hall, 1983, p. 8).*

The title and opening quotes that set the scene for this chapter come from Polly Walker as she reflects on the cultural and world-viewing dimensions of Peter's story in the previous chapter. Before moving to Polly's commentary however, we will pause and consider the very brief glimpse into the world of John Diew, currently writing from Sudan, but at that time, working alongside Peter, with the South Sudanese community in Brisbane.

Responding to Peter's story and reflecting on my bi-cultural role

John Kor Diew

Between August 2002 and August 2005 I was employed as a bi-cultural community worker in a Brisbane agency. Within that role I was involved in co-working with Peter along with some other colleagues in what we understood as a community capacity building project with the Sudanese community in Brisbane and Logan/Gold Coast areas. This project was identified by Sudanese community members as an initiative that needed on-going support. The project involved facilitation of mixed and separate workshops with young people and adult groups of Sudanese community with the intention of trying to narrow down the inter-generational gap that existed. The following reflections will mainly focus on my role in this community development project.

Building community capacity

The community capacity building project aimed to help build family and community capacity to deal with issues of inter-generational conflict and other related settlement issues. The main focus was on early intervention and prevention approaches to help families and community deal with issues before they become serious problems.

From my perspective this is done primarily through community involvement and giving community the chance to think about the issues of inter-generation and what solutions they can put in place to deal with it. It is all about giving support, promoting a 'can do' community spirit and helping families and community develop support networks and skills they need to deal with this issue.

My role

In the process my role was as a bicultural worker – for I am both Australian and Sudanese. I was assigned to clarify issues, goals, methods and experience from what can be seen as a 'verbal folk-lore' of the Sudanese people. This would enable me not only to benefit from mutual experience but also play a brokering role in sharing the knowledge and perspectives of the Sudanese groups with other ethnic groups and mainstream Australians.

In some of my informal consultation with Sudanese people many would see me as a source of information and expertise and would want to get more from me whenever opportunities struck. However, I saw the whole exercise and our relationship as more than that. It was two-way traffic whereby the members of the Sudanese community in Brisbane and myself benefited mutually. Even though I shared with them a considerable amount of my personal experience, one should sincerely confess that, what I have learnt from them was quite a valuable experience.

In all my dealings it is important as a worker to come forward as both professional and a friendly person. However, being a part of Sudanese community outside my work, it is quite challenging to keep the balance. I am always careful that my personal position should not affect my genuine position as a professional and an employee. It means that there are lots of difficulties that I must swallow in order to stand the test of being a genuine worker. The worker comes as a friendly, knowledgeable outsider who can be trusted to give advice without attempting to impose and who does not have 'an iron in the fire'. The worker can be adviser or consultant but must somehow not be a part of the group's conflict. Since conflict is mostly present, and is a natural part of any development process, and since each community member will have a part in that conflict, this is very challenging for the community member who is also worker.

Throughout the community capacity building project I constantly reminded myself that my role as a member of the community and worker at the same time required balance. My actions and decisions should not override any decision made by the community members. This put me in a difficult position if community members agreed upon a course of action that I did not agree with. It was such a difficult role to play but I managed to live with it throughout the life of the project. It became clear to me that it is important to have staff debriefing following any workshop or community process.

I also saw my role as recognising and supporting the Sudanese community as an established body. I was therefore able to work in collaboration with Peter in changing the character of the services being offered to the group. This shift from a focus on services to individuals needed to also include support from a community development perspective that would enable the communities to organise themselves.

Moreover my views regarding the outcome of any activity undertaken would often differ considerably from that of my colleagues. I believe this is due to my position as a member of the group and my interaction with the community outside work. I always think I have a clear picture of how things should be. Community members had their ideas – especially about young people. Colleagues often had different ideas. It was challenging to let community members and my colleagues at work share together, and it was hard to get all of them to work together as a unit, each contributing his/her best toward the achievement of the harmonious and safer community and families.

However, I learned to balance my sense that I knew better than most of my colleagues with an understanding that both my cultural perspective and theirs might need to shift to find some common ground.

Only a Sudanese worker?

In my professional community development work I often found myself in situations where others could not see me in any role other than that of a minority worker. It was difficult to become involved in mainstream issues because I was seen as having expertise, or an interest, only in minority issues. However, toward the end of 2004 my colleagues (including my line manager) came to realise that my skills and knowledge were adaptable and transferable to many other issues and that gave me an opportunity to work more broadly. Not allowing all individuals, from whatever background, to contribute their best impoverishes the organisations and limits them in achieving full potential as an organisation, as individuals, and as society. I felt limited until I was given permission to work with groups other than Sudanese.

Self-care

Part of my work in community development involved listening to the history of people I was working with (if they were willing to share them with me). Usually most of these people share the difficult histories of their flights and persecution they might have experienced prior to leaving their home country. They also often shared the difficult conditions and nightmare experiences they lived within refugee camps and during the first six months in Australia. All their histories were real and important too, however the most important of all is the feeling of loss and not knowing what to do after arriving in Australia. Being of refugee background myself I often related to many of their histories and their histories usually brought back to me some bad memories. This is important to be aware of so bi-cultural workers can take care of themselves and receive support from within their organisation.

Conclusion

My experience leads me to conclude that community development is an ongoing learning process whereby all can benefit equally. It is important that organisations employ workers from the communities they are working with, but care must be taken when working with any community developmentally. What seems an obvious way to approach things from an organisation's perspective, may seem to a community as if it will further harm their families and their community. Dialogue will not necessarily prevent this, but it can help people understand and support each other better.

A Sense of a Whole Other World: Worldviewing and Ethical Collaboration across Social Worlds

Polly Walker

In this reflection on Peter's chapter, I explore the growing body of knowledge on worldviewing, or the navigation of the deep rivers of culture. I discuss what worldviews are, how we come to practise them, and why they are such challenging concepts to understand. I also describe some examples of worldviewing in a peace building framework, designed to decrease violence and increase understanding and collaboration between members of different cultural groups.

In reading Peter's chapter, I found myself reflecting on 'worldviewing', on the ways we understand, experience and negotiate our realities and our social worlds with the realities and social worlds of others. Peter explains that a practitioner's analysis determines what he or she can **hear**. Many worldview scholars maintain that a practitioner's worldview determines what he or she can see and that developing more effective worldviewing may improve a practitioner's ability to collaborate across cultural difference in ethical ways.

My worldviewing experiences began as a small child navigating between a number of cultures. I am of Cherokee and Settler descent, and grew up near the Mescalero Apache reservation in New Mexico. Although I had no words to describe what I was experiencing as a child, I had many interpersonal encounters that troubled me, which I would now describe as worldview conflicts. As an adult, I became an administrator in the school system near that reservation, and found myself becoming increasingly distressed over the ways in which the school system ignored Mescalero Apache students' experience and ways of being in the world. Based on this concern, I applied for a research grant that would allow me to learn more about less violent ways of educating Indigenous students. I was awarded a fellowship which I took up at The University of Queensland, where I immersed myself in a study of reducing epistemic violence, the marginalization or suppression of a people's way of knowing and of being in the world. Since that time, I have had opportunities to interact with a number of scholars who specialize in working collaboratively across deep differences in people's cultures, who specialize in worldviewing within a peace building framework.

In this chapter, Peter describes his growing awareness of 'a sense of whole other world,' of the non-Western ways of knowing and being which he encountered in his interactions with members of the South Sudanese community. Worldview scholars would describe this moment of awareness as the beginning of developing effective worldviewing: the acknowledgment that our ways of being in the world, our values and beliefs are radically different than others' beliefs and ways of being, and understanding that working collaboratively across those differences is vital to us all.

What is a worldview? Edward T. Hall (1983), an anthropologist who wrote several seminal works on ethical cross-cultural communication, describes worldview as: "the underlying, hidden level of culture...a set of unspoken, implicit rules of behaviour and thought [which] controls everything we do. This hidden grammar defines the way in which people view the world, [it] determines their values" (pp. 7-8). In other words, a worldview represents the way a cultural group makes sense of the world and decides how to act responsibly and ethically within it. According to Jayne Docherty (2001), in order to develop an understanding of a group's worldview, we need to understand how members of the group would answer the following questions: 'What is real or true? How is the *real* organised? What is valuable or important? How do I know about what is? How should I or we act?' (p. 51). Answers to these questions comprise one's worldview, which has also been described as shared commonsense, or the deep 'assumptions that individuals and groups hold about the world' (Avruch & Black, 1991, p. 28).

However, we cannot learn about a people's worldview simply by asking them direct questions. Most people cannot fully explain their worldview verbally, because worldviews reside in the out-of-awareness level of our lives. The answers to the questions above are lived (Docherty, 2001, p. 51). We learn about our group of origin's worldview through experiencing situations within our group, and through exploring life's emotional, physical and spiritual aspects. We also learn through aesthetic experience, through stories, movies, and artistic works that explore a wide range of our group members' experiences. The ways we learn about our own group's worldview provides a map for learning about the worldview of others: through shared experience, dialogue, art, poetry, music, and story.

Worldviews are complex, multi-faceted and hard to understand partly because they reside in the out-of-awareness aspects of our experience. They are also challenging to understand because they are constantly changing and constantly being re-negotiated by members of a group. Indeed, a number of worldview scholars explain that it would be more accurate to say that we practise worldviewing rather than to say we have a worldview, and as we interact with others in worldviewing, we collaborate with them to view or make the social worlds in which we live (Docherty, 2001, p. 52).

When many practitioners reach the point of understanding that worldviewing involves the 'out of awareness' aspects of our experience, and that worldviews are constantly changing, they often place the process in the 'too hard basket' and continue their practice as if they can 'cut across' cultures with their professional techniques. However, ignoring differences in worldview both causes intercultural conflicts and exacerbates existing conflicts between groups, disrupting or destroying the collaborations that community workers seek to create.

We may learn more about another group's worldview when our worldview conflicts with theirs, and we are faced with the realisation that members of other cultural groups have a quite different view of what constitutes respectful and ethical behaviour. Indeed it is often the beginning of an effective worldview analysis when we begin examining situations in which our worldviews are not easily negotiated with those of others, when interactions across cultures result in discomfort or conflict.

A worldview conflict is one in which there is a strong element of negotiating over reality, including what constitutes ethical behaviour (Docherty, 2001, p. 53). Peter describes a worldview conflict in his narrative when he explains how several South-Sudanese elders challenged the service agency's largely Western approach to service provision. These elders expressed concerns that the resettlement services were fragmenting their families even further, in part through marginalising Sudanese cultural and community resources that could assist in keeping families together. The service providers felt an ethical responsibility toward fostering individual healing and wellbeing, which at times meant supporting an individual's desire to leave the family. This scenario is an example of a worldview conflict: behaviour that is considered ethical and appropriate in one worldview is considered to be disrespectful and disruptive when viewed through the lens of another culture. In this narrative, South Sudanese worldview placed a value on relationships characterised by sustained family networks. In contrast, the service agency's worldview emphasised individual wellbeing. In the language of worldview scholars, this is a conflict based on worldview differences between Sudanese collectivist culture and Australian individualist culture. To a large extent, members of collectivist cultures primarily value group harmony and relationships, and members of an individualistic culture privilege individual accomplishment and wellbeing (Hofstede, 1984, p. 167).

To transform conflicts such as this, members of both groups need to develop a clearer awareness of their own group's worldview as well as to develop an understanding of the worldview of the other group. It may seem obvious that people would understand their own worldview, however people are often not aware that they are functioning in ways that promote dominance of a particular reality, rather they assume that is the way all humans behave, or should behave (Galtung, 1996; Hall, 1977, 1983). In contrast, people who are members of a marginalized or minority culture must daily deal with conflicts between their worldview and that of the dominant group, and in the process become more aware of their own embedded worldview as well as that of the dominant group (LeBaron, 2003, p. 19).

Developing the ability to see through the lens of one's own culture, as well as to see, at least to some extent, through the lens of cultures of others, is a central aspect of worldviewing. However enhanced, worldviewing does not necessarily mean that the increased understanding of other cultures will be used in ethical ways. Some scholars and policy makers have been accused of using increased understanding to gain advantage over members of another cultural group. In order to transform conflict in ways that are respectful of all involved, worldviewing needs to be implemented within a peace building framework.

Peter's work with the South Sudanese community is an example of worldviewing within a peace building framework, in which it is not enough just to understand one's own worldview and that of another group. Ethical collaboration is also required. Worldviewing held in a peace building framework addresses many conflicts through people working together to rebuild what has been damaged or destroyed.

I believe that when Peter talks about his and the South Sudanese community's 'rebuilding of social worlds' he is describing an example of worldviewing in a peace building framework. Peter and the South Sudanese community leaders developed collaborative processes of working to rebuild the damaged social world of resettled refugees. The dialogical processes they instigated exhibit several principles of ethical worldviewing: The dialogue welcomed movement and change, and sought to avoid the dangers of attempting to freeze Sudanese cultural resources at some point in the past. They also avoided the trap of assuming that worldviewing is so challenging that collaboration is impossible (LeBaron, 2003, pp. 33-34). Peter and the South Sudanese community also engaged in the four basic principles of peace building delineated by John Paul Lederach (2005): 1. Relationships - enhancing the capacity of groups in conflict to imagine themselves in a collaborative relationship. 2. Paradoxical curiosity - refusing to be limited by either/or ways of thinking and living, instead seeking ways to bring 'seemingly contradictory social energies' into commonly shared goals and aspirations. 3. Supporting the Creative Act - embracing the possibilities for moving beyond the often narrowly and rigidly defined and accepted range of options, and 4. Willingness to Risk - creating spaces that give birth to the unexpected, new and creative processes and relationships (pp. 32-39).

Although fraught with complexities and challenges, the on-going story of Peter's engagement with the South Sudanese community provides insights into the role of ethical worldviewing. Such practice stories instil hope that community development workers can engage with people from different cultures in ways that are ethical, culturally sensitive and that promote healing, and encourage positive growth both in practitioners and the people with whom they work.

Editor's Transition

One of the things about Peter's story, along with other stories in this book, is that the work is not constrained to a particular role or organisational setting. Peter's commitment to working with the Sudanese community preceded the role that he is in at the beginning of the story. It probably began from relationships built through playing soccer with new arrivals in his community, and it was no doubt enriched by shared meals and social activities. When it became clear to him that his own and his organisation's role needed some new theorising, he made a decision to approach this through further study. This provided a context for a different kind of ongoing engagement with the Sudanese community. The PhD journey provided space to structure the dialogue with the community as well as with the organisation. Boundaries then are fluid. Di Zetlin became part of the new journey, as Peter struggled to find modes of theorising that were adequate to the experiences of himself and community members. Di comments from that position of co-traveller in theoretical realms and PhD supervisor.

Discovery and dialogue: a reflection on a community development PhD

Di Zetlin

My involvement with Peter's work is constituted by a relatively brief period in which I was part of the supervisory team for his PhD. In this commentary, I focus on those elements of the PhD process that seem to me to provide some resonance between his doctoral studies and community development practice. After a brief contextualisation, there are two themes I hope to isolate. The first is to identify a 'discovery', that moment when the horizon shifts and the view of that part of the world we have been certain we recognise looks different in some fundamental way. The second is on the dialogic process that happens between theory and practice in a thesis whose empirical grounding (or data if you like) is community development practice. I want to conclude with a few suggestions about possible extensions of this work.

Meeting Peter

In most discussions on how to do a PhD, there is often reference to the research journey (Clegg and Gall, 1998). This journey can be relatively straightforward, if lengthy. For example, a particular theory that works in certain contexts might or might not apply in a different context. This journey is based on the proposition that we know our way from A to B, and we can hypothesize that this well travelled road will take us to C. But there are other PhDs that follow much more uncharted paths. Peter's thesis was of the latter kind. His journey arose from a practical professional need to rethink practice in the light of 'client' critique. It started with that critique, but ended refashioning that critique into possible new models to ground intervention.

I met Peter first when he had already begun his PhD. In a sense the doctorate was incidental to the main purpose, which was to resolve an ethical impasse that had arisen from his professional practice. To be precise, despite years of professional practice, his interventions were being critiqued by the 'clients', the Southern Sudanese community in Brisbane, as contributing to their distress, rather than alleviating it. Ethically bound by a 'do no harm' principle, there was little choice but to step back and reflect on this diagnosis.

Peter's early discussions about his PhD reflected this commitment to an 'action research' project that would, in a sense, document the critique emanating from Southern Sudanese refugees about their engagement with human service professionals. The PhD would be a 'witness' to the negation of existing practice in the voice of the Southern Sudanese.

It became a very different exercise on the way to develop potentially new models to ground community building with (at least) resettling refugee groups. In a 'straightforward' PhD, the role of supervisor is akin to mentoring; providing support, encouraging focus, suggesting new initiatives, helping to keep track of time and task management, being a friendly critical reader. When the task is more complex, more inductive, the supervisor is a bit more like a co-navigator on the journey; trying to make sense of the map, debating whether this turn will take us to our destination, at times encouraging the exploration of off-road sojourns, at other times seeking to rein the journey in to its closure. The journey of Peter's thesis was mapped out in our periodic 'whiteboard sessions'. Where has the thesis come from, what have been the critical stops on the way, how can we make sense of this or that possibility, would A or B or C theory help here or there? At times wandering into areas where there seem to be no maps or the maps don't make sense of the environment, how can we chart a path forward? A frustrating process, I am sure, for Peter as the driver and chief navigator, but in the end I think a recognition that I have some little skill in cartography. In what follows, I try to identify what I thought were the most significant elements in the way Peter traversed his doctoral terrain.

The role of discovery

The early process of Peter's thesis was mapping the negation of existing practice that came from the Southern Sudanese community. It led into what became the turning point for the thesis because it enabled Peter to make a 'discovery'. Without delving into academic labyrinths to discuss the meaning of discovery, there is a common sense understanding of a form of discovery that is finding something that had been hidden from view. Usually, in retrospect, it appears so obvious that you kick yourself for having been so blinkered by your own perspective. In Peter's case, the 'discovery' was the insistence by the Southern Sudanese that their distress was temporally in the present rather than in the distant trauma of war and geographically in their resettlement rather than in a distant homeland. This is not to deny the trauma of war or the longing for home, but to insist that for a resettling refugee, making sense of the already constructed social construct of the 'refugee' and acting within, or against, in the foldings and at the boundaries of this imagined reality to create a hybrid community: this is the most critical locus of distress.

This 'discovery', simple as it seems now, was important because it allowed on the one hand, a deconstruction of the paradigms that most refugee community building work was focussed around. Deconstruction suggests a dismantling as if this can be done with bare hands. In fact deconstruction always rests on the concepts and theories of others in much the same way that one would hardly approach the deconstruction of a building without the use of powerful tools and engines. To record a narrative of distress in the words and experiences of the Southern Sudanese is one project. To deconstruct how that narrative has been produced and is in reaction to a given set of constructions of Western therapeutic constructs needs the theoretical work of people such as, in Peter's case, Bourdieu, Furedi and others.

On the other hand, the 'discovery' of the nature of the distress called forth a new part of the journey around 'healing'. This became the primary focus of Peter's dialogic or elicitive encounter with the community in the second half of his thesis. Out of the trauma of present distress, it became necessary to theorise how healing might take place in the wounds of cultural and social dislocation and trauma.

Theory/Practice

I was saved the details of many of Peter's interventions in and with the Southern Sudanese community and his attempts to explore his developing models with practitioners in professional development workshops. Where I was not spared was in seeking to capture the theoretical voices that resonated with those experiences. The dialogic or elicitive process placed Peter in the middle of a web of practice and theory. There were many of our 'whiteboard sessions' to secure the strands of this web and to launch it into its next orbit of sense making. What emerged was a model of social healing derived from a theoretical corpus around the concepts of culture, community and power and grounded in the experiential veracities of cultural practice, community praxis and the building of political efficacy or empowerment.

Two things stand out about this process. In the first place, it was theory as much as the engagement with the Southern Sudanese community that made it possible to discuss social healing as a process. There are times when practice based professions eschew theory. All that is needed is for the researcher/ practitioner to be 'reflective' in their practice and, perhaps, to acknowledge that they have a positional stake in the research 'object'. What follows is a research 'product' that claims legitimacy. My observation is that in the best research, theory stands behind reflection in its revealing moments. The second observation is related. In the case of Peter's thesis, it was theory that brought Peter back into the thesis. At a certain point, where he began to feel confident in his theoretical grasp of the concepts of social distress and healing, the 'conversation' with the community became less dependent on Peter as the listener and recorder. It assumed a more dialogic form. In short, theory enabled Peter to postulate possibilities that were not necessarily given to him at face value or in the negation of disciplinary practices that the narratives of distress told by the Southern Sudanese.

This commentary is based on a limited perspective as an academic. Peter's thesis was judged well by academic examiners. Ultimately its real judgement lies in whether social healing is a construct that is useful in dealing with communities in distress. I was never entirely satisfied that the model of social healing that Peter developed could address abiding wounds of gender. I also felt there needed to be a more complex analysis of the relationship between healing and the efficacy of relations of power. But then, remember, this was just a very small slice of a much longer story of community development.

Conclusion

In this chapter people who have been part of Peter's journey over the past few years bring added breadth and depth to an already complex landscape that has shaped the possibilities and constraints of the work. Again, we are reminded that we journey with others, who do not always agree with us, and who are shaping their own understanding of the terrain, holding together elements of their own history and experience. The support, wisdom, insight, and worldviews of our co-travellers are vital, as is their critique of our work. In this collegial process, we are each holding bits of a whole, that none of us can fully see, all becoming more than we currently are.

References

Avruch, K. & Black, P. (1991). The culture question and conflict resolution. *Peace & Change, 16*(1), 22-45.

Docherty, J. S. (2001). *Learning lessons from Waco: When the parties bring their gods to the negotiation table.* Syracuse, N.Y: Syracuse University Press.

Hall, E. T. (1977). *Beyond culture.* Garden City, NY: Anchor Press.

Hall, E. T. (1983). *The dance of life.* NY: Anchor Books.

Hofstede, G. (1984). *Culture's consequences: International difference in work-related values.* Beverly Hills, CA: Sage Publications.

Galtung, J. (1996). *Peace by peaceful means: Peace and conflict, development, and civilization.* Oslo: International Peace Research Institute.

LeBaron, M. (2003). *Bridging cultural conflicts: A new approach for a changing world.* San Francisco, CA: Jossey-Bass.

Lederach, John P. (2005). *The moral imagination, the art and soul of building peace.* Oxford: Oxford University Press.

Chapter 7
The Search for Invisible Cities

Community Development through the Looking Glass

Fiona Caniglia

'It should be people before bricks and mortar'. Gordon Fredericks[1]

This case study recalls the struggle of an inner city community to successfully influence a government driven program of urban renewal spanning more than 15 years. The inner northeastern suburbs of Brisbane (Queensland) were home to many of the city's remaining boarding houses and other low cost private rental housing. As urban renewal unfolded, disadvantaged residents faced displacement as lower cost housing was demolished, making way for higher cost apartments, up-market shops, cafes and restaurants. Public land was sold and industrial land uses were relocated to help facilitate renewal and urban consolidation outcomes. Despite the provision of some public and community housing in the area, overall supplies of lower cost housing have declined, rents have increased, public space has diminished, community orientated small businesses have

---

1.Gordon Fredericks was a vocal advocate of low cost housing and social diversity in New Farm. He was a founding member of NAG and died soon after leaving New Farm in early 1997. He is remembered in a monument to his passion – a bronze soap box in the form of a milk crate, at the corner of Welsby and Brunswick Streets New Farm.

disappeared and the cost of land has escalated. While goals such as urban consolidation are important in terms of sustainability, the urban renewal process struggled to deliver equitable outcomes to those already disadvantaged by low incomes and by processes such as deinstitutionalisation which left vulnerable people reliant on privately run boarding houses and hostels. New Farm Neighbourhood Centre worked with disadvantaged residents to ask the question 'what will happen to us?'

Background

In 1991, a program of urban renewal was announced by Lord Mayor Jim Soorley from Brisbane City Council and Tom Burns as Queensland Minister for Housing and Local Government (Urban Renewal Task Force, URTF, 1991, p. 1). The Urban Renewal Program was made possible through Federal funding under the Building Better Cities Program (BBC) and was to be administered by the Urban Renewal Task Force[2] (URTF) (URTF 1995, p. 2). Urban Renewal in Brisbane's inner northeasternern suburbs encompassed New Farm, Fortitude Valley, Bowen Hills, Teneriffe and Newstead, and aimed to attract at least $4 billion in private investment to better utilise otherwise derelict urban land and increase the inner city population (URTF 1995, p. 2). At that time, the area was described by various stakeholders as socially and culturally diverse and included a significant proportion of Brisbane's remaining boarding houses[3] (Boarding House Action Group, 1997).

Even though federal funding for urban renewal was tied to outcomes relating to social justice, it quickly emerged that disadvantaged residents on low fixed incomes were vulnerable to displacement as boarding houses, low cost flats, blue collar employment and low cost retail options gradually disappeared.

In early 1994, I was employed by New Farm Neighbourhood Centre[4] (NFNC) as the part-time community development outreach worker (25 hours per week). I was asked to focus on improving the level of participation by disadvantaged residents within the urban renewal process.

---

2. The Urban Renewal Task Force was structured as part of Brisbane City Council. Overall funding came from across the levels of government.

3. The Boarding House Action Group used available listings to identify 201 boarding house or hostel premises in the inner north which had declined by 76 premises to 125 between 1991 and 1996 (1997:17).

4. NFNC's target area included all of the suburbs that were part of urban renewal.

About urban renewal in Brisbane

The stated goals of the Building Better Cities Program were to encourage better urban planning and management by all levels of government, to result in:
- economic growth and micro-economic reform
- improved social justice for the less advantaged
- reform of inappropriate and outmoded institutional care for people with disabilities and the frail aged
- ecologically sustainable development
- more liveable cities.

(Campbell, 1993:272)

For Brisbane's inner north east, the specific goals of urban renewal included the following:
- to revitalise the area
- to implement urban consolidation
- to improve employment opportunities, access to facilities and housing choice in the area
- to improve coordination between levels of government and the private sector to increase the private sector's participation in inner-city development.

(URTF, 1994:L2)

Part of the structure of the Urban Renewal Program was a URTF Executive consisting in the early years of planners, development industry representatives and public sector representatives from each of the three tiers of government (URTF, 1996, 1998, 1999). The following table illustrates the composition of the executive and shows a gradual increase in the number of private sector representatives:

Table 1: Constitution of Urban Renewal Task Force Executive 1996, 1998, 1999.

	1996	**1998**	**1999**
Task Force	Lord Mayor Chair of URTF	Lord Mayor Chair of URTF	Lord Mayor Chair of URTF
Private Sector	Property Council of Australia Australian Institute of Valuers and Land Economists Brisbane Development Association	Urban Development Institute of Australia Brisbane Development Association Property Council of Australia Royal National Association Australian Institute of Valuers and Land Economists Australian Property Institute	Urban Development Institute of Australia (2 representatives) Brisbane Development Association Property Council of Australia (2 representatives) Royal National Association Royal Australian Planning Institute Australian Property Institute
Commonwealth Government	Department of Housing and Regional Development.	-	-
State Government	Department of Transport Department of Local Government and Planning.	Department of Transport Department of Local Government and Planning	Queensland Transport Department of Communications and Information, Local Government and Planning
Brisbane City Council	Local Councillor Department of Development and Planning Urban Renewal Task Force (Manager)	Urban Management Division (2 representatives) Urban Renewal Task Force (Manager)	Urban Management Division (2 reps) Urban Renewal Task Force (Manager)
Local Community	-	Local Councillor	Local Councillor

Source: URTF, 1996; URTF, 1998; URTF, 1999.

Community organisations and residents were never granted the right to hold positions on the Urban Renewal Task Force Executive structure despite ongoing advocacy by organisations such as NFNC. This diagram shows that in 1996, the local Councillor was categorised as a representative of BCC. While NFNC advocated for direct community representation, it was the local councillor who was eventually categorised as the community representative in the Urban Renewal Annual Report in 1998. While there is no doubt that the local councillor was a champion of many causes in common with the community sector, the composition of the executive reflected increasing private sector participation and only served to accentuate the relative position of the community in influencing the scope, direction and outcomes of urban renewal.

This is not to say there weren't numerous public consultation processes and events. URTF funded a Community Participation Team which operated a shop front in a central location and utilised a wide range of creative methods for engaging community members about their views about urban renewal (Community Participation Team, 1992). Even quite early in the process the Participation Program concluded that, 'there remained entrenched barriers to participation for some sections of the community'. (Community Participation Team, 1992, p. 4)

The Urban Renewal Task Force in relation to specific planning processes, also put in place a range of consultation processes including:
* meetings
* precinct committees
* charrettes[5]
* tours
* interviews
* street stalls
* submission processes to substantive documents such as social plans and development control plans
* newsletters.

There were many consultation processes and NFNC worked with local residents to ensure attendance and involvement. Despite this, there was a gradual realisation that consultation events were very different from opportunities to engage in ongoing participatory governance where residents and community sector representatives shared similar roles to private sector representatives and where real influence over outcomes was achieved.

It should also be recognised that the area strategy for Brisbane's inner north east stated outcomes including specific and detailed reference to social justice (Building Better Cities, 1991, pp. 13-14). For Brisbane's inner north east, these outcomes included consultation and participation, particularly relating to the most disadvantaged residents, the development of a detailed social plan, maintenance of at least the same stocks of low cost housing, employment and social diversity.

It was encouraging that the final social plan for New Farm/Teneriffe Hill summarised the following as key issues named during the community consultation process:

5.Charrette is a term used to "describe any intensive, group brainstorming effort" (Communityplanning.net website, 2009: http://www.communityplanning.net/glossary/glossary.php#design%20charrette).

- loss of low cost housing, particularly boarding houses and rental accommodation
- changes to the existing social mix as a result of gentrification processes, resulting in loss of social character overall
- fragmentation or loss of the existing sense of community
- loss of identity of neighbourhoods, human scale development and heritage values
- overcrowding and the resulting pressure on community facilities and services.

(Urban Renewal Task Force, 1994b, p. 13)

This list certainly reflected the issues and concerns of diverse stakeholders and reflected the concerns that NFNC was hearing from residents[6]. It was somewhat reassuring that a key document published by URTF was consistent with the views expressed by residents, particularly those experiencing the negative impacts of renewal.

Beginning tales

The community development outreach position had been vacant for two months when I started and there wasn't actually someone in the position to hand over any ongoing work. There wasn't much written that I could find – my filing cabinet included an overfull file labelled 'unsuccessful funding submissions' and a completely empty file called 'policy'! Members of the management committee were very supportive, however, and worked hard to explain their concerns about the exclusion of disadvantaged residents from policy processes and outcomes such as urban renewal.

Henderson and Thomas (2002, p. 43) outline some of the stages and steps in neighbourhood work which have helped me to reflect on the meaning and significance of how a worker enters the community, builds trust and negotiates a way in – particularly if there is 'deep suspicion'. In many ways I felt as though I ran the gauntlet! New Farm was a carefully guarded community and between a handful of well-meaning and determined residents, my first year was consumed with numerous attempts to find 'a way in'. As New Farm had been extensively 'consulted' over many different waves of public policy, some residents were naturally concerned about how I was going to work, and in whose interests. I definitely spent the first year in my role as an outsider. One local boarding house resident in response to my own reflections about over-consultation, wrote:

---

6. These were not confined to people who were being displaced but were also being expressed by residents from many different social and economic circumstances. For example, many attended community consultation events to express their concerns about the loss of low cost housing.

You mention that the New Farm people were over-surveyed. In addition, many of the surveyors over-promised and rarely returned with even a summary of their findings.

Joe Neal

One particular example of the challenges of negotiating entry as a worker centred on a funding submission I worked on under the direction of the management committee. The purpose of the submission was to better re-source the Centre's work to improve the level of access and participation in urban renewal processes by disadvantaged residents (Caxton Legal Centre, 1994). Although the submission emerged from the Centre's relationships with people being displaced by redevelopment, some other residents expected to have a very direct say on the scope of a submission and questioned whether extra funding was needed. This was a time of great conflict and even with clear evidence of need and a very involved management committee, the processes of trying to resolve the issues while continuing to build relationships and trust, were incredibly challenging. The events that transpired included quite public discussion of the weaknesses in my practice, which at the time seemed almost insurmountable and even a reason to withdraw and resign.

I felt like Alice in *Through the Looking Glass*:

> "Now then! Show your ticket child!" The guard went on, looking angrily at Alice. And a great many voices all said together..... "Don't keep him waiting, child! Why his time is worth a thousand pounds a minute!" .... "I'm afraid I haven't got one...there wasn't a ticket office where I came from."

(Carroll, 2008, p. 56)

While a chorus of criticism echoed around her, "the guard was looking at her, first through a telescope, then through a microscope, and then through an opera glass". At last he said, "You're travelling the wrong way". (Carroll, 2008:56).

It was clear to Alice that "the first thing to do was to make a grand survey of the country she was going to travel through". (Carroll, 2008, p. 53). "It's something very like learning geography," thought Alice(Carroll, 2008, p. 53). In community work terms, it was an important process of 'getting to know the neighbourhood' (Henderson and Thomas, 2002, pp. 53, 56). I was acutely aware of needing to build a picture of the area – the people, the leaders, the issues, the history; and I was also putting a lot of time and energy into trying to build relationships with residents. So while trying to negotiate a way in, build trust and develop some relationships, I was also trying to understand the territory in front of me and develop some idea of which way to go, all in the context that low cost housing was under rapid redevelopment with catastrophic impacts on people who were significantly disadvantaged.

Holding the bigger picture: critical social analysis in the context of front line practice

The urban planning system is critically concerned with the allocation and use of space that in turn is dependent on land. Kilmartin et al. (1985, p. 66) cite Castells in analysing that:

> ...space is as much a product of class relations and of the characteristics of modes of production as it is of any political or economic phenomena....capitalist societies will have a spatial or ecological form consistent with the production, consumption and exchange requirements of capitalism.

> (Kilmartin, 1985, p. 66)

Smith (1988, pp. 7-8) identifies the issue that exclusion, and unequal access to housing markets is brought about through zoning and land use controls. Fischler (1998:676) writes that 'segregation by zoning was not an aberration or an unfortunate mistake. It was an explicit objective, rationally pursued', and goes further to say:

> because proximity to people of a lower social status diminished the market value of property, the stability of prices depended on the preservation of safe distances between socio-economic and racial groups.

Stilwell (1986, p. 62) does consider that Australian cities have unfolded in a 'class-biased manner'. Because much urban development:

> has been undertaken by capital in the direct pursuit of profits, the community as a whole has borne the external dis-economies associated with unplanned development.....(and) where the state has been directly involved in shaping the form of urban expansion, it has tended to share the same pro-growth ideology and has accommodated itself to the forces generated by the capitalist system.

Caulfield (1991, p. 209) proposes that a coalition of interests from within both the public and private sectors works to maximise development and therefore their own interests in the city. Caulfield challenges that both private and public sectors are 'speculators in spatial stuctures' and emerges to ask the question 'what is the relationship between this coalition and public policy?' (Caulfield, 1991, p. 210)

There was considerable evidence of the public/private partnerships that were a product of the Urban Renewal Program. Developers promoted opportunities for investment that were linked to programs of public funding (Balderstone Hornibrook, 1994, p. 1). Published materials from the URTF also highlighted that the role of the taskforce would be to facilitate at least $4 billion in private investment (URTF, 1998, p. 6).

Barely beyond the announcement of plans for urban renewal in Brisbane's inner north east, Gill (1991, pp. 24-25) warned that:

> ...the central weakness is a form of planning which leaves matters to the market and the decision on who obtains a scarce position to the ability to pay (with) the core problem of allowing the market to decide is that the already powerful and privileged are the most likely to benefit.

One illustration of the escalation in land values is the James Street Precinct. 'In 1995, it was an old industrial area dominated by the Coca Cola bottling factory, with land priced at $250 a square metre. By the time they sold out in 2005, it was $2520 per square metre' (Williams, 2007, p. 1).

The challenge of language

There had been signs that the trend towards gentrification was unfolding earlier than 1991. Some stakeholders remain convinced that gentrification just happens – "it is a product of market forces that no-one is in control of......and it is part of the natural evolution of cities – something of a *natural wave*[7]."

This language implies that the opportunities to act are limited because what is natural is right and not able to be influenced. It was certainly the kind of language that some key stakeholders used to justify why their role in solutions was limited. It also functioned to limit the extent that people believed they could influence the outcomes, which further impacted upon levels of participation in consultation processes.

Instead NFNC held the analysis that government sponsored renewal has a huge impact on the strength, speed and scope of gentrification. The Urban Renewal Program was an intervention and as such could be actively shaped towards more equitable outcomes resulting in a community that remained socially and culturally diverse.

It seemed amazing then to read Italo Calvino's fictional account of a conversation between Marco Polo and Kublai Khan:

> ...... my empire is made of the stuff of crystals, its molecules arranged in a perfect pattern. Amid the surge of elements, a splendid, hard diamond takes shape, an immense, faceted, transparent mountain. Why do your travel impressions stop at disappointing appearances, never catching this implacable process? Why do you linger over inessential melancholies? Why do you hide from the emperor the grandeur of his destiny?

> And Marco answered: "While at a sign from you sire, the unique and final city raises its stainless walls, I am collecting the ashes of the other possible cities that vanish to make room for it, cities that can never be rebuilt or remembered. When you know at last the residue of unhappiness for which no precious stone can compensate, you will be able to calculate the exact number or carats toward which that final diamond must strive. Otherwise your calculations will be mistaken from the very start."

(Calvino, 1974, pp. 48-49)

The result of urban renewal processes were many 'stainless walls' yet also a definite 'residue of unhappiness'. This quote really captured the conversation we were trying to have in this process – with some stakeholders asserting that urban renewal was simply 'splendid'[8] and our concerns at what was being lost, seen by some as 'an inessential melancholy'. It was as though

---

7. This is a direct quote from a key stakeholder involved at the time.

8. The 10 year annual report for the Urban Renewal program included "10 years of success" on its front cover (URTF, 2001).

Marco Polo really understood the depth of sadness in collecting ashes from other cities that can simply never be rebuilt.

Listening to stories

At the same time as building an analysis and working to 'negotiate entry', I started speaking to residents. I spoke to anyone who would talk to me and in particular sought people who were being displaced because of the re-development of boarding houses and other types of low cost accommodation.

The stories brought to life the impressions of the management committee that the area was changing and that some people were particularly vulnerable to the negative impacts. One resident living in a boarding house posed the question 'what will happen to us' and set the tone for stories NFNC collated into a response to the draft New Farm / Teneriffe Hill Social Plan (1994).

> *I've just settled down...I thought I wouldn't have to move again...it's happened to me before...* Felicity

> *I've always been on the move, but this is the longest time I've ever spent in one place - I've been here nine months – so it is really good, I've started to settle down...* Steam Engine

> *We need to make people a heritage, not just buildings....people are an asset to the community...irrespective of their background, they always have something to offer...* Thomas

> *It is hard for me to get around. I've got a mother who needs looking after and I can't leave her alone for too long on her own, so getting to meetings would have been hard. (If I went) I'd stand up and tell them exactly what I thought of everything...* Felicity

> *When I go to meetings, I sometimes feel that I can't talk fast enough. Some people hear my voice and it puts them off....I would need someone to pick me up and take me home...* Cathy

> *We can't stop the government...whatever we say is not going to make a difference. They are just going to do it anyway...* Felicity

> *Life is fine here, everything is fresh...the children can breathe fresh air...I can't bear to see the trees go...if the rent was not so high we could stay.* Suzie

> *At one time they had a long term relationship with people and the place has been suddenly uprooted and they have to reform friendships and relationships...it is very traumatic...at times it is heartbreaking. It is the comradeship that is important, not the four walls...It is obvious if people live in little boxes then people never come into contact with each other, to their detriment. Without human contact you die...you don't talk you might as well die...To be in isolation from everyone....they would die emotionally...they would require more services, more looking after...we have fourteen people here and eight nationalities – we have lots to talk about.* Thomas

(New Farm Neighbourhood Centre, 1994)

Bringing people together

Having collected these stories, residents connected to the Centre together with the management committee and Caxton Legal Centre[9] , decided to hold a meeting in May 1995 to discuss the issues and what we might be able to do. A particular focus of the meeting was ensuring that local residents on low incomes were represented and central to any resulting structures or decisions.

At that meeting a group called the Neighbourhood Action Group[10] (with a convenient acronym NAG) was formed and decided to meet on a regular basis to have input to the formal consultation process conducted by the Urban Renewal Task Force. NFNC contributed resources and support to NAG through my position as a community development outreach worker.

NAG met regularly and decided on a set of strategic issues to focus on including:
- the loss of low cost housing and associated impacts on social diversity
- achieving universal access within spaces and buildings
- the impact of land use on social justice outcomes.

(New Farm Neighbourhood Action Group, 1996, p. 7)

Understanding the planning system was a definite challenge for the Centre and for NAG. The Centre was also struggling to sustain its work to engage more disadvantaged people in the planning process. To meet the challenge of developing formal responses to development control plans the Centre:
- sought funds from Brisbane City Council to achieve increased capacity to engage disadvantaged residents
- engaged our own planner to assist on a short term basis
- asked URTF to run training sessions for NAG members.

While working with these challenges, NAG was struggling with consolidating itself as a group. There were moments of conflict and sometimes it even felt as though things might fall apart. While members shared some common concerns, there was also many differing opinions and vastly different life circumstances. Building and sustaining the group highlighted how much diversity actually characterises geographically defined neighbourhoods. This was a definite strength but also a challenge as we worked to be effective against development processes over hundreds of sites fuelled by significant private investment and a planning system geared in favour of private property rights. These complexities highlighted the significant

---

9.Caxton Legal Centre was located in New Farm.

10.An earlier structure called the New Farm and Teneriffe Residents' Association was also heavily involved in development control activities.

challenge of working from a sense of 'I' to 'we', from 'me', to 'us' (Kelly and Sewell, 1988, p. 62).

Through a combination of formal processes (meetings, workshops) and informal time together (meals, gatherings), we emerged with submissions to the development control plans (DCP) that reflected in detail the culmination of community concerns over several years. These submissions also attempted to reflect the scope of what was possible within the planning system while edging as much as possible towards a vision for the future. We were often told that the planning system couldn't achieve what we aspired to achieve yet despite this, drawing lessons from other jurisdictions and our expert friends, we arrived at recommendations that were definitely beyond the scope of the existing Brisbane Town Plan. These recommendations included:

- the inclusion of a local advisory committee in the development assessment process
- more integrated development assessment processes with involvement from social planners
- targets for housing affordable to people on low incomes and a definition of low cost housing focused on housing that costs no more than 25% of income[11]
- bonuses and incentives for the retention or expansion of low cost housing
- disability access guidelines
- a community facilities plan.

(Heywood, 1995); (New Farm Neighbourhood Action Group, 1996)

URTF responded to two submissions by NAG to the DCP with comprehensive written documents which were well received by residents. Of greater significance was the inclusion of some of the following provisions in the New Farm and Teneriffe Hill DCP which were consistent with our recommendations:

- low cost housing was defined in the plan as able to be rented or purchased by people on low incomes such as pensions and benefits, and not exceeding 25% of income
- bonuses and incentives such as greater building height and gross floor area as well as reduced car parking requirements if a component of low cost housing was included in a development.

(BCC, 1996)

---

11. There had been contentious debate over definitions in the context that projects with residential units for sale were being promoted as "affordable".

A clearer focus on structures

While relationships are often identified as being at the heart of community, our circumstances made it clear that structural capacity was also really important. That is because many formal structures made urban renewal possible and we needed to understand and work with those structures effectively. We also needed our own structures to support our work.

The formation of NAG was in recognition that a shift from individual stories (as they were told to NFNC) was needed towards bringing people together and then creating a structure through which we could identify our goals and work towards achieving them.

After the gazettal of the DCP, to some extent, we thought our work was done and in the context of various resource constraints, NAG met less often. Almost exactly one year later, a meeting of community organisations and residents decided to form the Community Action Network (CAN) because of concerns about the actual implementation of policies like these. CAN was structured initially with four working groups each with one focus:

- coordination
- universal access
- low cost housing
- participation in planning processes.

The Centre provided continued secretariat support to these groups (convening meetings, keeping records, holding a library, research and writing resources for submissions, regular newsletters). The membership of CAN continued to include low income residents such as public housing tenants and boarding house tenants. However, it also included other residents and service providers in recognition of our shared concerns. It was also a deliberate attempt to include diverse local residents as a basis for communicating to government that these concerns were not isolated to low income residents but that there was a broad mandate to respond to the impacts of urban renewal[12].

In addition to NAG and CAN, we resolved to use every formal opportunity to participate. We didn't want our efforts to attract criticism because we hadn't held a place at the table in those mechanisms that were legitimised by decision making entities. At one particular all-day charrette, 10 NAG members were present out of a total of 45 participants. All of the NAG members present were living on low, fixed incomes at the time. We

12. Beyond the first couple of years of CAN's existence, it became harder to sustain a flourishing membership. A significant issue was the extent that many people thought it was a hopeless cause. A committed but small group remained involved in organising specific activities such as Twilight Training, Politics in the Pub and the CAN Awards, beyond the early years and this group became CAN-LINC during the Place Management project.

had done specific preparation prior to the charrette – reading and discussing the materials, refocusing on our concerns and what we thought the solutions might be. NAG members distributed themselves across all of the working groups on the day.

At the inception of CAN, the decision was made to refocus everyone's attention through a month of action, which included the following activities:

- Candle Light Vigil mourning people and places lost in the urban renewal process (attracting diverse residents – including those who had actually experienced displacement, those at risk of displacement and yet others who were concerned about the area's declining social diversity)
- a post card campaign highlighting the issues[13]
- Graveyard of Crosses to commemorate each boarding house that had been redeveloped
- media releases about our various actions
- a delegation to the Lord Mayor including proposals for actions and policies (with seven local residents in total including six people from either boarding houses, social housing, other lower cost private rental housing or whose income was derived from a pension or benefit)
- Politics in the Pub as an ongoing mechanism for discussing local issues in a way that also encouraged social relationships to develop and aimed at attracting existing and incoming residents from all demographic groups. Speakers, volunteers and those in attendance generally reflected the full social and cultural diversity of the area
- the inaugural CAN Awards Ceremony – celebrating government, business and community efforts across CAN's interest areas as a way of amplifying those initiatives in a way we hoped would inspire more effort particularly on the part of government and business. They also made us think seriously about the things that business and government were doing that contributed to social justice outcomes. Awards were given to people from every walk of life[14] and the organising committee reflected the diversity in CAN's membership. The CAN Awards have continued over 10 years.

CAN also decided to generate ongoing, community based training opportunities called CAN's Twilight Training to build the skills we realised we needed (if only in retrospect) including town planning knowledge, building and sustaining successful groups, being a successful advocate, working with the media and cultural competency.

---

13. These post cards were illustrated by Ron Muir, a local tenant in public housing who was a vocal advocate for housing issues and who is remembered since his death in the naming of a hall at New Farm Library. Ron was a committed member of CAN who also illustrated the certificates for the CAN Awards and was involved in many CAN activities.

14. CAN member Maida Lilley reflected that award recipients seemed genuinely touched about receiving an award.

We asked for a liaison structure between the Urban Renewal Team and the community as part of the initial recommendations from CAN in late 1997 and early 1998. BCC and URTF agreed to a structure called the Community Liaison Committee. This structure underwent some reforms before being discontinued in 2008 as the result of a Brisbane City Council decision. There were many significant challenges involved in shifting this structure beyond the level of a token. Nonetheless the Centre continued to contribute ideas and to engage with BCC about how the CLC could be strengthened up until the policy decision to end its formal role. At present there are no ongoing participatory governance arrangements between the grass-roots community and URTF with regard to redevelopment[15] .

Time, place, opportunity

While the urban renewal process ground on, other policy initiatives emerged that created opportunities for new relationships and structures aimed at mitigating disadvantage.

In late 2000, Brisbane City Council and the State Government started the implementation of a place management program in three designated areas including the inner northeastern suburbs.

The Centre was funded within the Inner City Place Project to convene local groups and networks to discuss and decide upon ongoing participatory structures that would enable the community to be more of a partner in decision making.

When Place Management came along we took opportunities to negotiate how some activities such as the CAN Awards and Politics in the Pub could be funded as part of a social capital strategy achieving mutually desired outcomes even if our language started out as different.

With Place Management funding, we deliberately worked to foster local leaders through CAN Twilight Training. The Centre's volunteer program also actively worked to engage local residents who took on leadership roles in the actual running of the Centre and in doing so, ensured that reception was staffed and the space able to be offered as a place of welcome to other local residents. The majority of volunteers were living in low cost housing in the local community and were reliant on low fixed incomes. The volunteer network itself represented a mechanism through which local residents became connected and built social relationships. Through the work of volunteers, training opportunities, Politics in the Pub and the CAN Awards, the Centre strengthened as a place of belonging.

---

15. The Council recently resourced a Community Participation Team consisiting of community, government and private sector participants to have input to the development of a Fortitude Valley Local Plan. The scope of this team was time limited despite continued advocacy by NFNC for an ongoing mechanism in recognition of the significant changes still to unfold in the area.

A pool of tears

Despite being a group of people committed to goals and objectives focused on social diversity and inclusion, we accumulated many disappointments including wave after wave of boarding house redevelopment where people were faced with the reality of displacement. CAN member and resident Maida Lilley recalled that some households were really pressured to sell so that sites could be amalgamated for higher density developments. Some residents from newer developments also became involved in challenging the rights of people on lower incomes to be in the area. 'People who moved in didn't always accept the people and the places that had always been here', said Maida.

For the Centre, the whole process of urban renewal generated a significant workload. In addition to working to influence the process involving local residents, many people from boarding houses and hostels came to the Centre for assistance to find alternative accommodation.

The way through was very much like Alice's reflection that:

> "I should see the garden far better," said Alice to herself, "if I could get to the top of that hill: and here's a path that leads straight to it – at least no, it doesn't do that"—after going a few yards along the path, and turning several sharp corners, "but I suppose it will at last. But how curiously it twists! It is more like a corkscrew than a path?"

(Carroll, 2008, p. 33)

Even when it seemed as though the path was going somewhere she found herself suddenly back where she started only to try again and again. It seems too close to the mark when Alice laments to the Queen 'you generally get to somewhere else – if you ran very fast for a long time as we've been doing' (Carrol, 2008:49). The Queen responded by saying that 'here you see, it takes all the running you can do, to keep in the same place. If you want to get somewhere else, you must run at least twice as fast as that' (Carroll, 2008, p. 49).

There is a certain bitter-sweetness to reflecting on this history in that other possible courses of action revealed themselves with a certain clarity that simply didn't exist in the middle of the furious pace of urban renewal. With so many sites under redevelopment our only hope seemed to lie in attempting to influence the policy framework. While this resulted in some measured outcomes such as the inclusion of recommendations in the DCP, we perhaps should have also focused on a couple of strategic sites where public land was being sold. It may have further served our efforts to have some strategic precedents where social justice outcomes were actually achieved and that were also a symbol of our sustained collective efforts. One CAN member reflected on this story as follows:

> Reading it made me aware of opportunities I had missed to urge the preoccupations of my boarding house community. Of course it is very easy to be smart in hindsight. The

period of your (my) growth in understanding of us coincided with my acquiring the tools needed to show others that we had valid aspirations......

As you know, I spent long hours at NFNC meetings practising patience and seeing the meeting as therapy in action. Now I see that I could have advocated some training on the lines of 'the meeting as a weapon' and 'how to use a meeting' or 'how to make sure it gets in the minutes'. Standing up and shouting for 15 minutes gets you nowhere. But writing it down, waiting till the last minute, standing up and saying it, and then handing the piece of paper to the Secretary, works wonders.

Joe Neal

I also realise in retrospect that I spent much of this time thinking about the situation with an 'us and them' mentality. While initiatives such as the CAN Awards attempted to break down these stereotypes on all sides, I can definitely see how I could have been more committed to relationships and dialogue throughout the whole process. Calvino (1974, p. 124) warned that when we cultivate 'the certainty and pride of (supposedly) being in the right' we actually stumble towards a 'malignant seed'.

These challenges also raise the question of how we sustain ourselves and our efforts and while elements such as supervision, peer networks, continuing education and balanced personal lives all help, the poor resources, long working hours and limited actual successes all take their toll particularly when there is a tendency to define this as an individual/organisational problem rather than a systemic issue.

Building the base

I only learned to start valuing my base when I began to understand its true power - the power of local people forming an association that added structure and capacity to their efforts to achieve change. Local people since 1981 had gathered in New Farm to create a more structured 'organised' base from which to work, giving themselves the legal capacity to attract and manage funds and a process for establishing a mandate for taking positive action at a local level towards social justice in processes like urban renewal. This was a community that had worked to be 'staffed' in the process of realising their hopes and aspirations and in the process of having influence.

I had to learn about the component parts of my base in order to consciously nurture it and like the Kublai Khan had to be convinced that 'without the stones, there is no arch' (Calvino, 1974, p. 66).

One of the interesting things about working in a context where several hundred sites have been redeveloped, is that you are confronted with various stages of the construction process – some sites undergo major excavation where you see the foundations being laid. These foundations then become invisible as the remainder of the process unfolds. It is obvious in the built environment that even though strong foundations eventually become invisible no one questions their importance. With this image in mind, the management committee and staff focussed on nurturing the base of this work in the following ways:

- documentation of extensive policies and procedures to support the work
- better articulation of the structure of the organisation into programmatic areas with goals and objectives as the basis for a strategic plan
- a clearer focus on how to attract sufficient resources to sustain those goals and objectives.

Looking Glass House: from base to place[16]

When Alice began to describe Looking Glass House to Kitty she said:

There's the room you can see through the glass – that's just the same as our drawing-room only the things go the other way.

(Carroll, 2008, p. 17)

She might have been talking about the house that is New Farm Neighbourhood Centre – a house much like any other house in New Farm with windows, doors, tables and chairs. The furniture and the rooms are in Alice's words 'quite common and uninteresting but all the rest was as different as possible'. (Carroll, 2008, p. 20)

The best physical sign that things 'go the other way' was seating in the front yard. It was a clear statement that anyone, anytime can take up a place and rest – spilling out into the public realm yet harboured safely in the entrance to the property – not hidden out of sight and out of mind, but a clear and visible statement of our intent – no matter who you are or what your circumstances, you can come here – and not only that, you can take as much time as you want. The Centre's Open House Program was designed to offer hospitality and welcome and was strengthened in response to the increasing pressure on public space and declining social diversity. Open House was an attempt to provide a range of things that gave a physical reality to being a place of belonging: tables, chairs, shade, a universally accessible entrance, a reception area with couches, books, papers, bottomless tea and coffee, internet access, a place where people know your name and if you don't come for awhile, someone to ask after you.

Even with all of the external changes and extensive redevelopment, the Centre's Open House response was built around the power of people knowing your name; the power of being missed; the power of having people to talk to and of being someone who listens to others. The power of having someone to be annoyed with; the power of having space to be and if you feel like it, to become involved; to do things with others that you believe are important at the same time nothing special yet very special, seemingly insignificant and often invisible to government, yet potentially very

---

16. Kelly and Sewell (1988) talk about space, base, place which has influenced my thinking here about these dimensions at the Centre.

powerful. With all of the considerable changes and threats to diversity, the organisation consciously gave time, resources and program status to the act of welcome.

Conclusion

Marco Polo said to Khan

all I need is a brief glimpse, an opening in the midst of an incongruous landscape, a glint of lights in the fog, the dialogue of two passers-by meeting in the crowd.

(Calvino, 1974, p. 126)

This says something to me about being able to seek and find even fleeting moments in which dialogue and listening are present as a basis for building community. Setting out in this way, with an eye for even the most fragile beginnings, may at least help us to sustain our practice in the context of such overwhelming odds. Sharing this capacity and encouraging the recognition of 'instants separated by intervals' seems especially important as the threats to building community continue to gather pace (Calvino, 1974, p. 126). If we face the prospect of few absolute successes, then let's amplify and celebrate 'fragments mixed with the rest' so that genuine efforts by committed people to build community embed themselves in our collective memory in a way that inspires us to try again (Calvino, 1974, p. 126). As Marco Polo says to Khan, we must *'not believe the search for it can stop'* (Calvino, 1974, p. 126).

References

Balderstone Hornibrook. (1994). *Teneriffe wharves: Brisbane's inner city riverfront address, the smart choice.* Brisbane: Balderstone Hornibrook.

Boarding House Action Group. (1997). *Inner city squeeze.* Brisbane: Boarding House Action Group.

Brisbane City Council. (1990). *Inner suburbs action: the strategy.* Brisbane City Council.

Brisbane City Council. (1996). *New Farm and Teneriffe Hill Development Control Plan.* Brisbane City Council.

Building Better Cities. (1991). *Area strategy – inner north eastern suburbs.* Canberra, ACT: Department of Housing and Regional Development.

Calvino, I. (1974). *Invisible cities.* Picador Pan Books.

Campbell, G. (1993). The Better Cities Program: A catalyst for urban reform. In Robert Freestone (Ed.), *Spirited cities: urban planning, traffic and environmental management in the nineties.* Sydney: The Federation Press.

Carroll, L. (1999). *Alice in Wonderland.* New York: Penguin Young Readers Group.

Carroll, L. (2008). *Alice through the looking glass: and what she found there.* London: Walker Books.

Caulfield, J. (1991). Community power, public policy initiatives and the management of growth in Brisbane. *Urban policy and research, 9*(4), 209-219.

Caulfield, J. (1995). Planning policy and urban development. In J. Caulfield and J. Wanna (Eds.) *Power and politics in the city: Brisbane in transition (Ch.9).* South Melbourne, Victoria: Macmillan Education Australia.

Caxton Legal Centre. (1994). *Local, vocal and focal.* Brisbane: Caxton Legal Centre.

Engwicht, D., Pitts, J. and Besley, J. (1992). *The Community Participation Team: an interim report submitted to the Urban Renewal Task Force.* Brisbane: Community Participation Team.

Engwicht, D., Pitts, J. and Besley, J. (1993). *Urban Renewal Community Participation Program: final report.* Brisbane: Urban Renewal Task Force, Brisbane City Council.

Fainstein, S. (1987). The politics of criteria: planning for the redevelopment of Times Square. In Fischer, F. and Forester, J. (Eds.), *Confronting values in policy analysis* (pp. 232-247). California: Sage Publications, Inc.

Gill, T. (1991). *Renewing the inner city: proposals for a Brisbane waterfront.* Paper for the Housing and Built Environment Conference, Chandigarh. Brisbane: Griffith University.

Heywood, P. (1995). *Submission to the preliminary draft of the New Farm/Teneriffe Hill Development Control Plan.* Brisbane: New Farm Neighbourhood Action Group, New Farm Neighbourhood Centre.

Kilmartin, L. et al. (1985). Social theory and the Australian city. *Studies in society (Series 26).* Sydney: George Allen and Unwin.

New Farm Neighbourhood Centre. (1994). *What will happen to us?* Brisbane: New Farm Neighbourhood Centre.

New Farm Neighbourhood Action Group. (1996). *Submission to the draft New Farm/Teneriffe Hill Development Control Plan.* Brisbane: New Farm Neighbourhood Centre.

Stilwell, F. (1986). State and capital in urban and regional development. In J.B. McLoughlin and M. Huxley (Eds.), *Urban planning in Australia: Critical readings* (pp. 49-66). Melbourne, Victoria: Longman Cheshire Pty. Limited.

Urban Renewal Task Force. (1991). *Urban Renewal Report: inner north eastern suburbs of Brisbane.* Brisbane: Brisbane City Council.

Urban Renewal Task Force. (1994a). *New Farm/Teneriffe social planning study background papers.* Brisbane: Brisbane City Council.

Urban Renewal Task Force. (1994b). *New Farm/Teneriffe Hill Social Plan.* Brisbane: Brisbane City Council.

Urban Renewal Task Force. (1995). *Brisbane Urban Renewal Report 1995*. Brisbane: Brisbane City Council.

Urban Renewal Task Force. (1996). *Brisbane urban renewal: 1996 report and five year overview*. Brisbane: Brisbane City Council.

Urban Renewal Task Force. (1998). *Creating people places: 1998 report*. Brisbane: Brisbane City Council.

Urban Renewal Task Force. (1999). *Addressing tomorrow: 1999 report*. Brisbane: Brisbane City Council.

Williams, S. (2007, November 17). Urban renewal an investment. In *The Australian*. *http://www.theaustralian.news.com.au/story/0,25197,2275 2058-25658,00.html*

Chapter 8
Another Perspective on New Farm Redevelopment

Pam Bourke

The first real signs of gentrification in New Farm began in 1988 when Brisbane's low-income residents in the inner suburbs were forced out of their housing to accommodate tourists at EXPO 88. At the time I was the Community Development Worker at the New Farm Neighbourhood Centre and we were confronted by many low-income residents seeking assistance with accommodation and tenancy advice.

Brisbane City Council had also decided at that time to implement the Inner Suburbs Action Plan, which was seeking to renew inner urban neighbourhoods especially where there were brown field sites that offered opportunities for redevelopment. The Neighbourhood Centre engaged in a lot of direct action at this time. New Farm is on the Brisbane River, and has some large wool stores, that were either disused or used as warehouses and temporary stores. The Neighbourhood Centre promoted awareness about the impacts of Expo 88, encouraged the community to request a greater say in the planning for the area, and supported opposition to the redevelopment for residential purposes of the wool stores. We supported the establishment of a residents' association to represent resident voices. We also collaborated with other likeminded people and community groups across the inner suburbs concerned about the social and environmental impacts of planning on communities. Action by these groups led to the establishment of the Urban Coalition.

I left New Farm in 1991 and joined Brisbane City Council in 1994 to lead the establishment of its community development teams. The four Brisbane City Council Community Development Teams (North, South, East and West) began in 1993. The Community Development Team West began early contact with New Farm Neighbourhood Centre in relation to the social impacts of urban renewal as a policy. Given the history of my work in New Farm I understood the importance of community involvement in ensuring that social issues were addressed in planning. In the community development teams we were particularly concerned about the loss of affordable housing and the impact on homeless people. A deliberate part of our work was to create opportunities for dialogue between the community and people in Council at a range of levels to highlight the need to consider social impacts and outcomes. We also worked internally to gather senior people around the issues and to offer support for integrated planning and community engagement.

There was a consciousness that we needed to work beyond an ideological approach. In other words it would not be enough to tell planners urban renewal was having negative social impacts on communities, we also needed to seek some practical ways of making a difference.

For those of us in the Brisbane City Council community development teams this was challenging, as urban renewal was by this time embedded in the organisation and politically and organisationally much more powerful than the community development teams. The approach to urban renewal was primarily driven by creating opportunities for profit from development as well as a commitment to urban consolidation and quality urban design. Despite references to social, economic and environmental outcomes, retaining socially mixed communities was not a high priority. The community development teams had very little leverage for change with the urban renewal team.

After several years of trying to influence urban renewal from the inside, we consciously changed tactics and actively pursued a parallel strategy through place management. The impacts of urban renewal were being evidenced in increasing homelessness and other associated problems around alcohol management and safety. This new approach required a coordinated government, community and business response. Place management was a policy that had associated programs and a budget. It was led by Council in three locations within metropolitan Brisbane based on levels of disadvantage and need. These areas were Carole Park, Zillmere/Stafford and the inner city (including New Farm).

Through place management we were able to encourage dialogue and build structures involving the State Government, local businesses, community organisations and residents. The dialogue and structures were geared towards exploring the issues and developing action plans that would guide the work in a number of areas including social capital, community development, community safety, employment and economic development, housing and homelessness. Place management also included a higher-level coordination group made up of government, business and community members.

Some of our work within Brisbane City Council was focused on enabling a range of stakeholders to take advantage of place management as an opportunity to progress their interests. Inputs included facilitation, secretariat support, community development activity as well as funding for other stakeholders to undertake a range of roles and functions. These inputs enabled many networks and structures to become focused around complex and entrenched local issues.

While some collaborative planning was involved, a strong focus was on enabling various stakeholders to actually do things together. This was in the context that considerable 'planning' had already happened yet the implementation of social planning outcomes was criticised by a number of stakeholders as being somewhat weak.

From a Brisbane City Council perspective, the community was often represented by staff from community organisations and also some higher profile community leaders who spoke on behalf of other residents. Funded activities enabled broader community participation in various activities including cultural and employment projects involving young people and social capital building activities such as the New Farm Community Action Network Awards and their Politics in the Pub. On reflection, perhaps more effort and resources should have been directed into involving more disadvantaged residents. Whilst the neighbourhood centre was engaged in this work, their efforts were not really visible to decision makers and bureaucracies and this had implications for how such work is valued and funded.

Brisbane City Council tried to be aware of existing, bottom-up agendas and to then utilise place management opportunities and resources to support them. It raised the question about bottom-up versus top-down processes and highlights that these approaches are not necessarily best understood within a binary framework. If the role of government and the community sector is recognised as different, then it becomes possible to acknowledge the importance of bottom up and top down processes occurring simultaneously. This requires an understanding by community organisations that government is not a unified entity. There are usually people within government agencies working for change who will welcome partnerships with the community. Council used its size and influence to also broker and leverage other contributions and policy changes particularly from the State Government. The place management approach was very fragile, however, and to have long term impacts required a shift in government coordination, planning and decision making that was not forthcoming in either state or local government.

The decision by the State Government in 2005 to inject significant funding for new initiatives, including funds to respond to inner city homelessness, was undoubtedly influenced by the place management project. However, soon after, policy direction changed in Council and support for a place-based approach diminished. Without Council leadership the place management approach was gradually dismantled. From a community development point of view, some significant and trusting relationships developed between stakeholders across different levels and sectors and this was a significant journey for everyone involved. This work demonstrates the importance of relationships across boundaries and how people working together from different perspectives and power bases can create change. It also demonstrates how fragile that change is if it isn't embedded in well-resourced independent local organisations that support the work in the community in the long term.

In hindsight, the work in New Farm raises the issue of how to balance the effort put into changing, or managing the impacts of government programs such as urban renewal with the support for capacity building in local communities. Building strong local participatory groups and organisations that are not solely dependent on government is essential if communities are to have a say in managing their future and continuing to find a place for those people who become the victims of so-called 'progress'.

Chapter 9
Reflexivity Looking Back–!

Ann Ingamells, Fiona Caniglia, Athena Lathouras, Peter Westoby,
Ross Wiseman

By way of conclusion, and recognising some of the inherent shortcomings of any attempt to recount the multi dimensions of practice, the editors determined to engage in some personal reflection on the stories. This process of reflection occurred in one session, and this final chapter is organised around the structure of that session. This is a somewhat unorthodox conclusion, but it is consistent with the unfinished business of making sense of our work.

To re-attune each person to the narrative that they had written some weeks prior, the session began with each person drawing an image to capture the main significance to them of their story. We created a number of questions about the narrative to be drawn randomly from a hat. These were aimed at what the narrative says, not what the intent of the practice described in the narrative was, although this was a difficult line to hold. So questions had wording like: what is the main image in my drawing; how do I constitute myself in the narrative; how does the image reflect tradition, and so on. In the session we worked with only three questions. They provide a sufficient, but not exhaustive base for reflexivity.

Each person spoke to the image they had drawn to represent their narrative. Ross had composed a vault – a large chest. The lock had been forced open and the people inside were scurrying to freedom. This depicted the desire at the heart of the narrative to free the spirits of older men whose life-force ebbs before its time when cut off from community life.

Fiona had drawn a boundary, inside which was space, representing the centrality of a particular physical place in her narrative. In this delimited space, she has used abstract symbols to indicate that all of the characteristics and attributes, drives and ambitions, pleasures and pain of people everywhere are present here. Through adding weight and contrast to symbols, she indicates that the impact of societal resources in this space is not neutral. Public money and institutional power can be applied for the good of all, to benefit the least advantaged, or to give license to the desire for power and money. Fiona provides three concurrent readings of the image. One is of relations between public servants, developers and local people, especially most disadvantaged local people. Another is about a new community development worker testing out her analysis, her understanding of method and her skills in a particular place impacted by a fast moving, highly resourced policy initiative. Third and most important is the question of how people can get connected to the place where they live, and to people in that place, in ways that provide a sense of belonging and continuity.

Peter's primary image was a journey. Journey, as movement across space, includes adventure, anticipation, tracts of darkness and disappointment. The journey of people leaving Sudan and arriving in Australia, looking to establish homes, community, and family life. The vortex of welfare hovers above them as they reach a certain point in the journey, sucking them away from themselves to a place where they receive some support, but never enough and where they become labelled as vulnerable, needy and traumatized. There is a bust up, a crisis, with sparks flying, as the newcomers reject this approach to helping. The journeys continue with Sudanese workers trying to negotiate welfare jobs; organisations trying to be more empathic; the Sudanese preoccupied with a range of settlement and family challenges, and Peter, embarking on a thinking journey - seeking to re-think the discourse of host country response to refugees. Meeting places in these journeys are rich spots of dialogue and they produce rich negotiations between cultures, but there is a long haul to get even tiny changes in a system of welfare that keeps reproducing a way of seeing and responding.

Ann's image was of stepping stones - safe spots, across a busy, somewhat threatening and consuming swamp. People are building safe spots together; reaching out across safe spots. Trying to stop the safe spots getting consumed by the forces of the broader swamp, they almost topple. They get pulled back; they peer forward, looking for spots of light to aim for as they negotiate the spaces between stepping stones.

Athena's key image is dynamism, as constant movement between levels, depicted as circles inside each other and a heart, as a kind of complex of values (sometimes coined under the umbrella of social justice), at the centre. There are people, places and stumbling blocks everywhere throughout the circles, and the circles themselves are shifting all the time.

Trying to get resonance with the heart at any level, means trying to get it at all levels, moving quickly, light on the feet, reading the shifts. Sometimes you cannot free the heartbeat from where you are, but if you shift sideways, a new possibility emerges. These intuitive shifts are hard to explain yet can be transmitted through relationships. This work is not for everyone, and it requires such a changing, often intuitive, reading of the possibilities that it is not easy for organizations, as they are currently constructed, to plan or manage or supervise.

This reflexive process brought home an already uncomfortable awareness of how monocultural the group is. Exposed here in the form and narrative structure is something of the heroic quest of western mythologies. Heroic quest narratives (consider The Iliad and Odyssey) tend to prescribe the roles and qualities of the hero or leader and over time, through novels, biographies, films and other narrative forms, this is consolidated as a discourse. It becomes difficult in western cultures to recount a story of struggle for change that does not enter this discourse. Yet, it is not the most helpful discourse for community practice. All narrative imaginations are inevitably formed within their cultural context. An Aboriginal or African storyteller would centre narrative round a quite different form, that would spell out quite different implications for actors. The narratives however, whilst recounting something of an odyssey, are not quite captured by the cultural discourse, as analysis of Athena's narrative form, below, suggests.

Athena's image shifts the focus from the linear notion of quest or journey to a more dynamic concentric and interactive notion. Where community workers may resonate to a central concept of social justice, they encounter, even in the same project, actors who imagine and resonate to different core values. Replace the heart with a dollar sign and different agents across public and private spheres are energized. Put in the centre, the nexus of social, economic and ecological balance of the triple bottom line and a range of different actors and actions are energized. The struggle is about determining what gets institutionalized as central values, and therefore what gets legitimized as public action, policy or law. The creative form in this narrative is permeable to a range of contradictions. Human beings act alone and together on what they value. This may not be the same as what they would want to see universally expressed in everyday life. Institutional values, possibly reflecting the majority weight in the social body, or perhaps where the power lies, will only partially reflect the different values of any particular group. Community development is presented here as a method of practice that intervenes in this valuing process, seeking to put social justice values at the core of public and everyday life. It does this both through engagement in particular places (community of place) or in particular groups (community of interest), and in public domains as they impact on these communities.

Fiona, however, through her introduction of Marco Polo into the narratives, anchors the recognition that the seeds of the unjust city are in the search for the just city, just as the excesses of the unjust city throw up a search for justice (Calvino, 1997). In Marco Polo's view, a diet of rice and celery soup and an avoidance of complication and excess (epitomising justice), begets the pleasure seekers and those who will have rich spices at anyone's cost.   If this is the dynamic on which societies exist, is it to change it that we intervene, or to access the excluded to its manifest choices, or to impose a democratic template over it, forcing some constraint and redistribution, or is it to destabilize pockets of entrenched privilege? Perhaps each of these strategies has its moment. Multiple strategies break the hold of the polarity or binary described by Marco Polo, but they take a lot of energy to sustain.

The next question in the reflexive process was: *How is self constituted in my narrative?*

Athena's immediate response to this question was 'as a leader'. Her narrative is about anchoring a set of values in the everyday roles, relations, policies, procedures and action strategies of an organisation. Incomplete as this might always be, nevertheless, the tasks of imagining the values and working with others to devise ways of instituting them even within a limited organisational and geographical sphere, is an act of leadership. Having claimed the leadership space, Athena then equivocated – 'does that sound arrogant? I mean lead from behind', I mean a promoter or demonstrator of these methods and values'. We knew what she meant! Gender conditioning and the humility of this community development tradition make it difficult to say, but leadership is required.

Fiona also saw self in her story constituted as a driving force, but more as broker than leader. The broker moves between people and institutions, trying to assist them to connect with each other. One aim is dialogue – a kind of conversation where each can speak, and each hears the other, and people are prepared to be affected by each other's situation. The second aim is that these connections get institutionalized in some way. The enormity of the task and the fragility of self, are a constant presence in this narrative. Rather than hold constant a presence to each other, the two sides remained fragmented, the residents slipping off as the heat came on, and the institutional players barely pretended to listen. The discontinuities were overwhelming, and the feeling of having failed, was never far from the surface.

Peter, reflecting on his narrative, also saw self as lost and stuck. Immersed in action that he thought was helpful, he was stunned by the eruption and critique of the people he worked with. This was especially so, as he had held that critique of welfare himself, yet had thought he had found a mode of practice that was different, more supportive, more engaging. Working with his organization to respond to the critique, a few changes were made: more consultation, a South Sudanese worker appointed, more dialogue. Yet the institutionalized forms of welfare discourse continue on their disempowering trajectories - individualizing, assimilating, labelling as vulnerable and traumatised, and undermining agency. Peter needed time to think, review, reflect, deconstruct, and he needed a mechanism of engaging South Sudanese people in that process. For him the time out was made possible through study and research, as another dimension of the change process, whilst nevertheless holding the relationships.

Ross saw self in his narrative as projectionist. He took Mike and Washuntara's story and projected it up large, so we all could see it, and appreciate its contribution to the whole. In similar vein, Ann at first expressed concern about being invisible in her chapter, but named the self there as chronicler. Both are valued roles, if a step removed from activist.

The third and final question that the group focused on was: *How does the image portray the relation to tradition?* Fiona takes the lead here, having had some years to reflect on her early practice experience. She says that her inexperience led her to focus on the wrong things. Residents, influenced by her approach, did not challenge the direction, or not in a way she could hear. Influenced by the particular tradition of community development, she interpreted her job as to engage local people in urban renewal so their voices could be heard and bring some influence. Her commitment to social justice led her to resist and fight against urban renewal and the development orientation associated with it. A third part of her struggle was that her reading of the policy materials on urban renewal led her to believe that the urban renewal actors should be using more democratic processes as espoused in the literature. These and possibly other factors combined, in her words, to produce a tendency *to get too focused in on their micro processes and on how to get them to a point where they could listen. We (the urban developers and the local residents' group) never got to a shared language, we (the residents' group) had very little power in public forums, and they (the public/private urban development partnership), although they needed the visible participation of local people, systematically overrode relationships and contributed to poverty that they refused to see.*

In retrospect, for Fiona, a different analysis could have produced more strategic actions and possibly outcomes that would have been more helpful to the least advantaged residents of New Farm: *If we had accepted more quickly that, given the convergence of government and developers, urban renewal was going to happen, we could have focused in on where the public land was, and how to secure some for community facility and affordable housing. This would have given a direction to our actions that developers and urban planners could understand, would have given a pointy edge to negotiations, and may have resulted in a more concrete outcome. We simply never thought of this as an approach. Some minor battles were won, but the community got less from the process than it might have.*

Reflecting on the relation between the image and the developmental tradition, Athena reflected that in her narrative, workers not residents, engaged in the policy processes. This shift to worker-centred practice, with the local residents no longer visible or active is a departure from the method of holding the people in, both through the local processes and through wider engagement with structural forces. She said: *I can see why we as workers go to policy forums rather than try and involve residents. Just because people want to change something that impacts directly on them, does not mean they want to live a politicized life, or dedicate the time and energy to the complex processes through which policy change or activism occurs. It is often just too hard for worker and residents to hold this dimension in. Workers try to hold in all levels, whilst residents work where they are willing and ready to.*

Fiona responded by saying *how mindfully we need to be in that space. We need to make it explicit that work continues across all layers and that people can move into other layers with you. As it is, people come to a couple of meetings, then they stop coming, and they feel guilty if they cannot stay in at all levels for the long haul. But decisions are made by those who are there, and workers can try and hold in the residents' interests, preferably with their knowledge and permission, but sometimes even in their absence.*

Peter added from his attempts to create dialogue with young people: *You begin a project, and there might be one hundred young people who are interested in participation. There might be ten who will want to participate in planning and leadership activities. Perhaps there will be four or less who will want to address the issues of space or funding, and go to see politicians or the Mayor. We don't all have to participate at each level on every front of our lives.* He added: *I might work with 100 young people in order to eventually get to working at more strategic levels/processes with a few people.* Everyone benefits from the joint activity. Some, who choose and are ready, benefit from other levels of participation too, like decision making, planning, strategizing, addressing issues, engaging with politicians, bringing about social change. It is these latter young people who get to know something about how the wider world around them works.

Ross's insight as he reflects on his narrative, is how much more was needed to secure the changes than he or others could possibly bring to it. *We did what we could, with the energy we had. We mobilized others where we could, and we secured what organizational assistance we could. We made some changes in people's lives, but to secure those changes in a way that would be sustainable and benefit a wider group, required so much more energy than we had.*

Nevertheless, it is when we act to change something in our world, that we gain our best understandings of how our world is structured, how power operates, and who we are in this. We learn as many workers and community members have, that next time we would do things differently because of the knowledge we gained this time. We also know, although sometimes it is difficult to put one's finger on it, that the world is a better place for ordinary people expressing that they care, through acting together.

At a more meta level, people reflected that practice is more pressurised within neoliberal contexts. Projects are fast moving, communities cannot keep up; everyone is under pressure to perform and to deliver outcomes; resources are always inadequate and timeframes too short. Yet, strategies are emerging to maintain a community focus. Where broader social change looks impossible, or requires more energy and resources than people can muster, then at least local islands of belonging and inclusion may be possible. Community building at the horizontal level will provide the grounds to develop analysis and therefore to foster community action, but at the community pace. Whilst the market may be the wrong distributor of opportunities and resources, communities are becoming players there. Continuing deconstruction and exposure of the discourses that subject people to isolation, disadvantage, vulnerability can provide one form of action and may lead to new and more varied community development strategies.

Even as this book was being produced, community groups have begun increasingly to restructure their operations to become players in the market. They have done this as a matter of survival, believing that they can at least hold in the most disadvantaged people in that way. These stories need to be told, reflected upon and learned from. That might be the book to follow this one.

This final chapter has demonstrated some of the human, personal and methodological struggle as well as the costs that at times accompany community development practice. Hopefully, some of the joy and commitment is also evident. This book has provided a brief glimpse into some of these realities.

References

Calvino, I. (1974). *Invisible cities.* London: Vintage.

Index of Words

A

accountability, 17, 23
action research, 58, 69, 82
agency, 4, 19, 39, 58, 62, 63,
  64, 65, 66, 67, 74, 79, 79,
  114
agenda, 8, 13, 15, 18, 19, 27, 43,
  63, 67
auspiced, 23, 42, 60

B

boarding houses, 85, 86, 90,
  94, 98, 100
bottom-up, 18, 25, 45, 109
bottom-up initiatives, 52
Brisbane City Council, 86,
  88, 95, 99, 103, 104, 105,
  107, 108, 109
Building Better Cities, 86, 87,
  89, 103

C

capacity building, 74, 75, 110
Caxton Legal Centre, 91, 95,
  104
citizenship, 11, 22, 27, 60
client centred approach, 52
collective inclusive approach,
  52
community action, 69, 116
Community   Action
  Network, 97, 109
community analysis, 15, 24,
  27, 66, 67
community based, private,
  public sector, 49
community development, 3,
  9, 9, 11, 12, 13, 14, 16, 16, 18,
  18, 19, 20, 21, 22, 24, 25, 26,
  28, 28, 29, 30, 31, 35, 36, 41,
  45, 45, 57, 58, 62, 63, 66, 67,
  68, 69, 70, 72, 74, 76, 80,
  81, 84, 86, 90, 95, 107, 108,

109, 110, 112, 113, 114, 115, 117
community planning , 12, 51
conflict, 31, 58, 59, 60, 62, 64, 65, 68, 71, 74, 75, 79, 79, 80, 84, 91, 95
consultation, 69, 74, 89, 89, 90, 93, 95, 114

D

developmental, 1, 3, 3, 5, 5, 11, 12, 13, 14, 16, 18, 19, 20, 22, 24, 25, 26, 27, 34, 38, 42, 44, 45, 63, 70, 115
dialogue, 2, 5, 13, 13, 14, 15, 34, 37, 43, 58, 58, 63, 64, 67, 68, 70, 76, 78, 80, 81, 101, 103, 108, 112, 114, 116
diversional therapy/diversional therapist, 38
doctrine, 49

F

frameworks, 14, 42, 64, 66, 70

G

gaining entry, 66
gentrification, 90, 93, 107
governance, 5, 27, 41, 42, 89, 99

H

healing, 57, 58, 58, 61, 62, 64, 64, 66, 79, 80, 83, 84
individualised, 63, 66
communal, 35, 68, 69, 70
heurisms, 14

holistic approach, 53
housing, 6, 40, 61, 66, 71, 85, 86, 87, 88, 89, 90, 91, 92, 95, 96, 97, 98, 99, 103, 104, 107, 109, 115

I

implicate-method, 15, 15
incorporated organisation, 50
institutionalisation, 33, 36
integral, 14, 16, 24, 27
intergenerational, 32, 62
invitation, 41, 59, 62, 70

L

labelling, 64, 67, 114
leaders, 58, 61, 63, 64, 69, 70, 80, 91, 99, 109
leadership, 23, 42, 43, 58, 61, 62, 63, 63, 67, 99, 110, 114, 116
crisis, 62, 71, 112
customary, 63
formal, 5, 23, 42, 43, 44, 60, 62, 70, 95, 96, 97, 99
informal, 23, 41, 61, 62, 63, 70, 74, 96
legitimate, 62, 67
legal compliance, 49

M

macro-method, 15, 15
managerial structures, 49
meta-method, 15, 16, 16
methodology, 67
colonial, 61, 67
neo-colonial, 61, 62, 67
mezzo-method, 15, 15
micro-method, 15, 15

Mohandas K Gandhi, 12
mutuality, 13, 15, 17 , 27

N

New Farm Neighbourhood Centre (NFNC), 86, 88, 89, 90, 93, 94, 95, 97, 101

P

participation, 2, 3, 5, 11, 32, 86, 87, 89, 91, 93, 97, 104, 109, 115, 116
Paulo Freire, 12, 14, 25, 67
place management, 6, 99, 108, 109
poverty, 3, 12, 16, 25, 26, 115
power, 2, 3, 4, 9, 12, 43, 62, 63, 84, 101, 102, 104, 110, 112, 113, 115, 116
privatised, 35
public space, 72, 85, 102

R

reciprocity, 27
Redland Shire Council, 47, 48, 54
reflexive, 64, 113, 114
residential aged care facility (residential facility), 39, 46
re-structuring, 63, 69
risk management, 6

S

sea-change phenomenon, 40
social change, 4, 8, 15, 20, 22, 24, 29, 41, 66, 116
social context, 67
social diversity, 89, 95, 98, 100, 102

social isolation, 21, 23, 29, 35, 37, 38, 40, 40, 45
social justice, 5, 17, 30, 31, 86, 87, 89, 95, 98, 100, 101, 112, 113, 115
social mix, 90
social movement, 5, 41
social plan, 89, 89, 94, 104
social practice, 47
social processes, 7, 58
structures, 2, 3, 4, 11, 15, 20, 35, 37, 41, 43, 68, 95, 97, 99, 108, 109
structuring, 16
Sudanese, 57, 58, 59, 60, 61, 62, 63, 64, 65, 66, 67, 68, 69, 70, 71, 72, 73, 74, 75, 76, 77, 79, 80, 80, 82, 82, 83, 112, 114

agency, 4, 19, 39, 58, 62, 63, 64, 65, 66, 67, 74, 79, 79, 114
community, 1, 2, 4, 4, 5, 6, 8, 9, 9, 11, 12, 13, 14, 15, 16, 17, 18, 19, 20, 21, 22, 23, 24, 25, 26, 27, 28, 29, 30, 31, 32, 33, 35, 36, 37, 38, 39, 40, 41, 43, 44, 45, 45, 58, 59, 60, 61, 62, 63, 64, 65, 66, 67, 68, 69, 70, 73, 74, 75, 76, 77, 78, 80, 80, 82, 82, 83, 85, 88, 89, 90, 91, 92, 93, 94, 96, 97, 98, 99, 100, 101, 103, 104, 107, 108, 109, 110, 112, 113, 115, 116, 117
community association, 58, 60, 63
Christian Fellowship, 60, 63
Elders group, 58
liberation, 12, 41, 60, 63
lost boys, 60
refugees, 17, 57, 59, 60, 64, 66, 68, 71, 72, 80, 82, 112
resources, 3, 5, 6, 8, 8, 17, 18, 20, 23, 34, 35, 38, 40, 41, 44, 65, 68, 69, 70, 79, 80, 95, 97, 101, 102, 103, 109, 112, 116, 117

women's association, 60
worker, 3, 15, 19, 20, 21, 22,
    42, 58, 62, 66, 67, 68, 69,
    74, 75, 86, 90, 91, 95, 107,
    112, 114, 115, 116
youth association

sustainable (as in sustainable
    service), 4, 18, 20, 20, 22,
    25, 27, 30, 48, 51, 52, 53, 55,
    87
systemic, 59, 68, 101

T

therapeutic, 21, 22, 57, 64, 65,
    66, 83

context, 2, 5, 8, 15, 26, 30,
    35, 36, 40, 58, 61, 65, 66,
    67, 68, 80, 81, 88, 91, 92,
    97, 101, 103, 109, 113

culture, 8, 32, 38, 40, 43, 61,
    62, 64, 65, 66, 71, 73, 77,
    78, 79, 83, 84
discourse, 5, 36, 66, 112, 113,
    114
interventions, 21, 57, 62, 81,
    83
orientation, 2, 2, 57, 61, 64,
    69, 115

trauma (traumatised), 64, 114

U

urban renewal, 85, 86, 87, 88,
    89, 90, 91, 92, 93, 95, 97,
    98, 99, 100, 101, 104, 105,
    108, 110, 115

W

worldviews, 77, 78, 84

www.ingramcontent.com/pod-product-compliance
Lightning Source LLC
Chambersburg PA
CBHW060044030426
42334CB00019B/2487